Oh, How

BEAUTIFUL YOU

Are To Me

REVEREND LINDA FAMBROUGH

Oh, How Beautiful You Are To Me

by Reverend Linda Fambrough

Published by One Faith Publishing

Richmond, VA

onefaithpublishings@gmail.com

Unless otherwise, noted all Scripture quotations are from King James Version (KJV) used by permission of public domain.

By the request of the author, syntax and sentence structure was not applied.

Table Of Contents

A Special Word from W. Graham Harvey, Jr.,

It has been my privilege to know Linda for over 20 years. She has a heart for the things of God and is serving Him with all her heart. One of the characteristics of Linda that has impressed me is that she has a bigger concern for what is best for the Body of Christ than the concern she has for the advancement of her own individual ministry.

She wants to see the growth of the Body of Christ in her city and is willing to give herself to that growth more than just trying to make her own ministry grow bigger.

Linda is one of the Lord's true servants. Whatever she has to say is for the benefit of the advancement of Christ's purposes and not her own (which, I'm sorry to say, is rare in the American church today).

W. Graham Harvey, Jr., Pastor

Crossroads Christian Fellowship

Hopkinsville, KY

A Special Word
from Doug Abner

I have known Linda Fambrough for more than 15 years. This book "Oh How Beautiful You Are" tells the story of a God-Chaser who has sought the Lord most of her life. An Encounter with the Lord at 12 years old put her on a path that would cause her to travel from place to place to seek God's Presence and His perfect will for her life.

One of those trips brought her to my town, Manchester, Kentucky the "City of Hope" which had experienced real community transformation. My first encounter with her showed me her intense desire to know and do the Lord's will.

I was led to pray for an anointing to come upon her to minister as a leader in Henderson, Kentucky and surrounding areas.

As I write this, our Nation is in a battle for our very existence as a Christian nation. The Church seems to be tossed and turned in every direction. We need REVIVAL desperately. However, the Good News is the Lord is raising up a radical remnant church that will see amazing things happen, in the midst of persecution. This remnant group of believers will be led by many regular everyday people who are sold out totally for the Lord. I believe Linda is one of those people.

May this book encourage you to press on to draw close to Him.

Doug Abner
Retired Pastor of Community Church
Manchester, Kentucky

Currently Co-Director of
110 Main Regional Prayer Centre
Manchester, Kentucky

Introduction

When the Lord spoke to me and said, "I WANT YOU TO WRITE A BOOK!" I was amazed, thankful, but I did not understand. Yet, I began to meditate, and think about what happened in my life. No, things did not turn out one hundred percent the way I thought, but God has been faithful.

The Bible says, *"Stagger not at the promises of God."* Still, somehow, I felt that was one of those moments when you don't have to understand. The Lord always knows what He wants from us and I have been willing to give Him everything. No, I am not perfect, but God is, and we can always know that His perfection can be found in our lives. My spiritual level is high in Jesus, and I know that I am a daughter of Zion because His love and His patience reside in me and I am straight as an arrow.

After working in the government place for fifty years, you learn where and how to move in different ways. So, inside of this book, I will put everything in this writing that He gives me. To God be the Glory!

As I returned from the service in Louisville, I was thinking about where I was at. A credentialed minister with Assemblies of God, and a Pastor of a rescue mission. Surprisingly, I had to pinch myself again. So humbled and satisfied. So thankful that I was able to share with my father, who had gone on to be with Jesus, that the Lord was going to use me. I prayed with my dad one day on our knees and he renewed his salvation, and it was wonderful.

That day has never come with my husband at this time, but I kept on moving. One thing my husband did do, he thanked me for all the work I did for him with the trucking companies, the bookkeeping, and all that was involved. Which was very kind of him.

I want to encourage any woman who feels they are called; God will make a way. Some husbands will not allow spiritual growth in their wives, which is wrong because women grow spiritually and follow Jesus just like men. My husband's mother was a Godly woman and had rules: prayer, no cussing, and a strong Bible reader.

My husband told me after we married that he thought I had money. Well, I did not have money, but I had something far more important, A CALLING. I thank the Lord that he now attends my services at the shelter, and I didn't even have to ask him to come. He just showed up one day after I started. Now, that is a miracle! God does increase your territory. I have now been allowed to represent God's business, as I have done what He asked. I want to walk so close, that He can whisper, and I will hear Him.

CHAPTER ONE

Mommy, Mommy, Mommy

I was born Linda Ann Brock on September 13, 1943. My family and I lived on Clay Street in Henderson, Kentucky and later on, we moved to Evansville, IN. I went to Stanley Hall Grade School for 2nd and 3rd grades; afterward, we moved to 522 2nd St. with my great aunt and grandparents.

We lived in one house with my great aunt and my grandparents lived next door. My mother took me to church on Sundays to the Central Presbyterian Church. My dad had been raised in the church, but he never went to church when I was growing up. My grandfather sang in a quartet and he also was the church secretary.

I've been raised with what I call a "God-consciousness" a Godly consciousness to know that there is a God. For example, my mother put a picture of Jesus on the wall of my room, and even though I can't recall any kind of Bible study, I do remember coloring pictures at church. When you are young, you don't think much about spiritual things.

One day when I was between the ages of five and eight years old, we had a very bad storm. It was extremely dark outside, but when the rain stopped, I went to the kitchen and decided that I wanted to step out onto the back porch and sit down on the steps and look out over the sky.

As I sat down on the steps and began thinking about the storm, the hard rain, and the dark black clouds they were still hovering over. I looked up into those black clouds and they began to separate as the sun's brightness and beauty just seemed to pop through the dark black clouds. The beauty was colors of red and yellow and all the colors of the rainbow, but it was very beautiful and strong, it was like heaven touching earth.

As I sat on the steps and looked up, I began to meditate on how this could be. How could this be happening with all of those dark clouds, that such a beauty can step through something so dark?

Do you know this is what happens when salvation comes into our lives? The old dark clouds that hang over a person's life does not have to stay. Instead, you can decide to be a receiver and receive God's mercy, but most importantly is receiving His overcoming power. An overcoming power that is given freely to all of us.

We must be set apart from the world and walk in that salvation to become joint-heirs with Jesus Christ, to become those kings and priests, and fulfill what God wants to fulfill when we give Him full reign.

As a small child, as I once was, you don't understand what true salvation is because you're too young, but the Bible says to come as a little child, and I will reward you openly. I never knew that beyond those clouds in the sky that there was such amazing beauty.

When we look up into the sky and see the clouds of the day, we don't realize that there are more beautiful clouds above it. I remember getting up to step on the porch and running into the house to my mother, who was in the kitchen saying, "Mommy, mommy, mommy, come and look, come and look!" We walked to the door and looked out, but I don't remember our conversation at that time. I don't know if she even saw what I saw because I was receiving it from God.

For me, it was like God was opening into my heart because there is no beauty like that here on this earth. It made a true impression, and even after speaking to my mother about that day over these last few weeks, my mother also remembered when I came into the kitchen from the back porch saying, "Mommy, mommy, mommy, I saw God!"

Yes, I saw God, and even though I didn't see Him face to face, it was as if the atmosphere that He dwelt in was right above me and I could see the beauty of heaven and where He resides. The beauty of God's atmosphere and the gates of heaven are more outstandingly beautiful than we can ever put into words. I truly believe that God had that day especially planned for me to be able to touch Him in a way that I cannot describe but I can see it today and I believe that He has covered me over my life with His beauty.

"I AM WITH YOU
AND I LOVE YOU"

As the years went by, I continued to go to the Presbyterian Church on Washington Street with my mother. We always had Bible school in the summer and usually had several children who came along. Some went to church there, and some of the children were from the community.

As I began to grow and reached the age of 12, church camp was available for us and those who wanted to go. I don't remember anyone from my church that went, except me, but I do remember riding in a bus to the woods nearby Kentucky Lake. While there, we had some that would sing, of which I was included. I have never been much of a singer; however, I always sang whenever the opportunity arose. What was so unfortunate for me, was that we practice our songs during the day and would have them ready for the service of the evening, and I was given a part to sing by myself.

As the service started, we all sang together until it came time for my solo part and I just froze up, which was very unusual because I do not have scary feelings, which is wonderful. I don't know if I just wasn't ready or the words slipped my mind, but this is what did happen; everyone hum the melody of the song and no one ever knew that the choir had a problem, and it sounded okay without my part.

The camp was for one week and there were different activities, and of course, different things were going on, like going on a hike. There were boys and girls at this church camp. I don't remember connecting with very many, but the remembrance of the hike is most vivid in my heart and mind. I recall hiking up a hill and it was like a dark dirt path, and as we were going up the hill, there at that moment everyone had gotten behind me or ahead of me and I was walking alone. As I continued up the path the Lord began to speak to me, it was very short, but it was very important and straight to the point. The Lord said to me "I AM WITH YOU AND I LOVE YOU."

Now being a 12-year-old girl, and not knowing about the Holy Ghost of which I was never taught because in the Presbyterian Church you don't hear a whole lot about that. It may have changed today but back then I did not know that the Lord could speak to you individually. I thought that the Lord was too holy to speak to people on the earth but that is when the Holy Ghost comes in to do the will of the Father.

I certainly found out that those words have been with me and they carried me over my life. I will never forget the words spoken over me. I have no doubt that it was God because He spoke of love and being with me. I do not feel that I understood faith at that time, but I knew that it was the Lord.

I went to my counselor and expressed my experience and she replied by saying that she thought it was time for me to join the church. She was very kind and knew I was speaking the truth to her, but she did not lead me to Jesus. When I returned and shared it with my mother and father, my father spoke up immediately and said that I was not going to join any church until I had tried the Baptist church.

My father had joined the Baptist church when he was young. He did not go to any church when I was growing up, but he was a true Baptist at heart. So over the next few months, I started going to the Baptist church on the corner from my house. My friends went there, so it really worked out well, but after a period of time, I began to feel conviction while in the church services. I did not know that you could feel conviction when you were not in deep sin, so I tried to be clean and live right.

The first boy I was serious about was a deacon at this church. We went to church together on Sunday night every week until he wanted more than I was willing to give; so, we separated ways. He came back to me after I had dated someone else for a while, but we just never got back together. As the conviction continued to fall, I went to my pastor and he said he thought it was time for me to join the church. So, I joined the Baptist church and got baptized and you always wore white to be baptized on that day.

I was a senior in high school when all of this was going on. I had been swimming at Atkinson's pool that day and after swimming, I went home in my bathing suit and coverup. My pastor's son came by to see if I could order some pans from him, as he was getting married and was trying to raise some money. I invited him inside and he laid the pans out on the couch for me to see. I was hot from swimming and my face was red. My father came in about that time and got very upset and blew it all up out of proportion. He thought I looked horrible and asked what I was doing. I told the guy that I could not buy any pans, and he said okay and left.

I was going through some other things at this time. After my graduation, I was contacted by Lockyears

Business College from Evansville. I was interested, but my father said we could not afford it. My father did not want to discuss this or even see what could work, he just said, no.

I was an only child, and he may have thought that I would stay home. I had a job after school at a Brokerage, and I was earning money to help with what I needed. My father was a car salesman, so I drove an old ford, but I was able to get around. My mother was very upset at how my father had acted in front of my pastor's son, and I couldn't attend Lockyears Business college was just more than she could handle. My mother threw up her hands and said, "Linda I am done!" and on that day, we are out of there.

TURNING THE PAGE

I can't even remember how it all came together or how we got to Evansville in an apartment; however, I do remember as we left on the bus that day, my mother handed me a stub off of our tickets and said. "Here's your ticket to a new life."

I did not know what that new life would be. We didn't have a car, so my mother walked to work every day because my father did not allow me to take the car I had been driving while at home. I looked for a job and finally got hired by my mother's employer. I worked in the advertising dept. and I was also a switchboard operator. That was a whole new thing for me, but I enjoyed it. I met a lot of good people; plus, in this job I helped to care for our needs.

During this time, my girlfriend in Henderson introduced me to a guy and we started to see each other pretty often. He ran a gas station and had to work but we worked it out. After being together a few months, he asked me to marry him. When he asked, he never said he loved me, and when I asked him about that he said, "Well, I asked you to marry me, didn't I?" When I told my mother, there did not seem to be a problem, but my father did not agree.

I met this guy's family. He had been raised on a dairy farm and quit school way before he should have. Well, I said, "Yes," and he gave me an engagement ring and got a job at Gibbs in Henderson. I did not ask the Lord about this marriage, but I did have some God-consciousness. When I spoke to his mother, she had a little Bible with his name in it and where he had received Christ.

My mother made an appointment for us to see the preacher of her church. It was not more than 3 to 5 minutes for each of us and the preacher agreed to marry us in the Presbyterian church. My father agreed to walk me down the aisle, and after setting the date for my wedding, my mom and dad set a date the next Saturday to remarry.

At that moment I knew that I was part of their problem. My dad agreed to start going to church after all those years of being with my mother. He took a very active role in the church, and they moved to a new church after joining with another group at the church on Main St.

So all seemed to be working out, BUT I DID NOT ASK THE FATHER ABOUT HIS PLAN. My earthly father got back in church and the beauty of it was that he gave the Lord his all. He did a good job and was well thought of. My mother must have said to remarry means that we go to church together. My father never brought up his Baptist roots and I had forgotten all about my Baptist roots too, and I stopped going to church.

Shortly after being married, I was offered a job as a personal secretary to the manager of WJPS radio in Evansville. WJPS was the largest radio station in the tri-state. I would make ONE DOLLAR an hour. This was the 60's and that was a decent wage.

My mother had moved back with my dad and started riding with a friend to Evansville to go to work. I do not remember how I got to work; except I guess I got a car, but I do remember parking at a curb close to the radio station downtown. I got to be on the radio for different things. One time was for a news broadcast, but my voice was not strong enough over the air; so, those times were limited. Still, I was ready to get to Henderson anyway.

My husband and I moved around from place to place for a period of time, which means, my husband went from one job to another. Then one day I was told the radio station had been sold and my job was terminated. I received unemployment until I was hired on at the

Industrial Uniform. That job was short-lived as I did not have enough tax and bookkeeping knowledge at the time. So I left.

At about this same time, I was called to see if I would be interested in a job at a veterinarian office. The owner lived in Marion, KY, and the Dr. that I would be working with was from Alabama. It seemed like it would be fun. I like animals, plus we lived on Marywood Dr. so I would be working across from Audubon Park. So the job was close to home.

After working with them for a few months, I began to see something that I really did not want to see. The vet was doing work and putting the charge in his pocket. The owner sent his main girl to see me each week, and after a week or two I told her what I was suspecting, and she told me to write down what I saw him doing and put what I felt should be the charge. After doing this I realized that there was very little money coming in and very little money going to the bank.

After I got the list, I began to realize how important this money was to the owner, and even though this vet was a partner, he wasn't the head man. I began to see that there was quite a bit of money that he was not turning into me.

No, I did not want to be held accountable. So after I made a list of a few pages over the course of the day I called up the vet. I had the girl from the Marion Kentucky office come and she came to see me every week on Wednesday and I was to make a list of everyone who came in for service.

The horse care was mostly done outside the building, and I could not hear or see any services that were taken place. However, with the amount of customers that were being taken care of and not turned in for the money, I told her, " I am sorry to tell you this, but I don't know what to do because I'm seeing money being put into this veterinarian's pocket and he is not turning it in." I gave her my list of the services done, and the best that I could estimate on what I thought the charges would have been. So, she went back to the owner's office in Marion Kentucky, and told him the story.

Now, the owner made a visit to my home one evening, and I showed him my list of customers that I suspected that the veterinarian was putting their money in his pocket and the owner said, "Okay, here's what I'm going to do. I'm going to give him three days to get out of town!" He told me that when I get to work, lock the door, answer the phone, and do what you can do.

During this time, I found out that I was expecting my first child, but I was at peace. After that incident, the owner decided to close the Henderson office and I was laid off. Yes, I was happy because with a baby coming this would be a perfect time to draw some money and be off.

My husband had taken over a drive-thru gas station and he would work days and close in the evening. For some reason, there was a girl who would come and sit with him during his shift for whatever reason. A few months after we purchased a house on Melody Lane, we were able to keep our horses behind the house, and I began decorating a room for the new baby to come and I had a wonderful time doing that.

I stayed home for a year after the birth of my first son and then I decided that I would go back to work. Within that year my husband changed to another service station with a friend to form a partnership. When my son was about 2 years old, I decided that I would have to go back to work. My husband never told me to go to work, but when you see you don't have enough to live, you know something has to be done.

One of my father's friends was the manager of the H&R Block office in Henderson and he asked me to come to work for him as a receptionist. I did, but the amount of business that came in was too much to carry. So, he asked me if I would care to take a tax book home and read it and try to start doing taxes. I said I would, but I don't know, but all I can do is try. I took a book home and read what I could read, and afterward, he placed me in the position of a tax preparer.

I had not been to school for a tax preparer, but I adapted to it; in fact, I enjoyed it. I must be a figure person because I like the people I worked with. The owner hired a new receptionist, and everything was good. God was bringing me into the knowledge I would need down the road because I opened up to tax work at H&R Block at that time.

After working there as a tax person, I went to the tax school the next year in Evansville and was asked to take over the Henderson office as the manager and I did just that. I was the manager there for a year maybe two, and this was when the tax returns were paper. I also taught the tax school the second year, and I taught tax school in Henderson for H&R Block. After that, I was offered a job as an administrative assistant over the tri-state, which covered everywhere from Boonville, Henderson to Newburgh and all the Evansville areas and I took that job.

After several years had passed, I found out that I was not a happy camper. I found myself having thoughts of wanting a good man for my son because his father had no God-consciousness; nor, did not he give a hoot about church or raising our son the way he should. So, I began to think that I needed to look for someone else, and thoughts about going out to find one, but I could not do it on my own. So after a little time, I let it go and decided that I would make it with God's help.

My uncle offered my husband a job in the coal mine at Uniontown, KY. It would be the best money he could make, but of course, it was more dangerous. We bought 25 acres of land earlier with a herd of cattle at Smith Mills, KY. We sold off the cattle and paid for the land and made plans to move there because it would be a lot closer to Uniontown. But it would take a while, and in-depth plans had to be made.

During this time, I showed quarter horses and had a beautiful sorrel quarter horse that my husband had broken for me to ride. We also joined a fast draw gun club, we had good friends and we were close. But it was not for very long as the Lord had other plans.

WHAT WOULD IT TAKE TO MOVE THE HAND
OF GOD IN YOUR LIFE?

_____

_____

DO YOU WANT TO HEAR WHAT THE LORD
HAS TO SAY?

_____

_____

DO YOU REALIZE THAT YOU NEED HIM OR
DO YOU FEEL THAT YOU DO NOT NEED
ANYONE?

_____

_____

ARE YOU CONFUSED ABOUT WHAT YOU
BELIEVE?

_____

_____

A NEW DAY

While we lived on Melody Lane, I felt convicted about not being in church. I felt unsatisfied and I just knew that there was more for me and more for my family. I felt that we needed to do better when it came to things of God and so I started going to a Baptist Church where my husband's family was attending.

The preacher came out to our home to speak to my husband about attending church but to no avail. No way would he agree, I had it in my heart so strong, but what I couldn't understand is why would a man that is so blessed and has things, be so ungrateful and really not caring about anything.

Why wouldn't he want to go into the house of God?

Why wouldn't he want to go where other people are believing and having the Spirit of God upon them?

Well, I guess it was because he had to work, and he had to provide. So, I started going and I took my son, who was about four years old. It was nice to be there with my husband's family. I went to the preacher one day and I told him, "I have been in church all of my life until I got married and I just cut it off, and now I am in a position where I am not a happy camper. I know that I've got to get everything back in good order with the Lord. I've got a child, a son that I want to have Jesus and I will not settle for anything less."

The preacher said let's kneel down in his office, and he prayed for me in the most special way that I have ever seen in my life. There was a freedom that saturated my life and the dark cloud that hung over me was released, and that beautiful sunshine began to shine once again. Afterward, the teaching in Sunday school was the beginning of Genesis, the first chapter. Yes, it was a New Beginning for me, and I did not know that the Baptist preacher had received the Holy Ghost.

The Bible says you shall receive power once the Holy Ghost has come upon you. I had never been taught, and the preacher never shared it with anyone. However, he did go to a prayer group with people who had been put out of the Baptist church. One couple was my best friends, my husband and I use to ride motorcycles with them. We had not been with them for a while, so I was glad to see them when they began to come to our church occasionally.

So, this wonderful pastor prayed for me and I saw the fruit from his prays but I also saw power. I did not hear him speak in the Holy Ghost, but he prayed for me and I saw immediate results. God knew exactly what I was in need of, and I learned so much at that time. I didn't know of a Holy Ghost, I only heard it when some would say in the name of the Father, Son, and Holy Ghost. Well, they put this precious pastor out of their church, and it would be a terrible loss for them. Afterward, I started going to another Baptist church at Reed, KY and I began making new friends.

My motorcycle friends and I were very close at one time and we had an awesome friendship. Everything was good, but I did not know until later that they were beginning to reach out in ministry on their farm. God had touched their lives and my dear friend invited me to a women's prayer group at her home in Corydon, KY. So, on Tuesdays I went, and we studied the Bible. It was a nondenominational group and there were probably about 10 or 12 of us because she had reached out to draw her friends and neighbors. Friends and people that were interested in the Word of God.

This was the beginning of The Sheep Shed Ministry. One Tuesday when we were there and everybody had left but me; this is when my girlfriends and my best friends began to share with me about the Holy Ghost with the evidence of speaking in tongues, which was a heavenly prayer language.

> » *Did you know that the Holy Ghost can come upon you and you will pray in a language?*

> » *Did you know that you can have a prayer language in the Holy Ghost of God?*

Well, I never did. I had never heard of it, and I had never heard anyone speak about it because you don't hear about this in the Presbyterian or the Baptist Church. That's all I have ever had growing up. I said no, I have never heard, and they said to me,

"Do you want to receive the Holy Ghost with evidence of speaking in tongues as the Spirit given utterance?

"I certainly do, but I said I don't want to hear it. I don't want you all to pray it out loud to me. I don't want to go home and make up some mistake. I want the real thing. The real deal" I replied.

"Okay. We will not pray out loud but we're going to pray and lay hands on you and pray for you to receive the Holy Ghost, and you'll receive your prayer language," they said.

I said, "Thank you, Lord!"

My friends prayed for me and said, "Now, if you get a little syllable of a word, go ahead and just say it over and over, it may take a little bit of time You might receive it fast or in a few days."

I left the house, and as I was on my way home, I got a little piece of the word, but I don't remember what that piece of the word was; yet, I said it over and over and over, and whatever else came across my heart to say. I said the words regardless of what it was or what it sounded like because foreign languages were unknown to me.

Several days went by, and I was home one day making up the bed. Everyone had gone to school and work, and while I was home by myself my prayer language in the Holy Ghost began to flow. I flowed in my prayer language and fully received the baptism of the Holy Ghost with the evidence of speaking in tongues.

When you receive the Holy Ghost you will always have the evidence of speaking in tongues. So anyway, I was just beside myself, knowing that God had honored me once again, and I had received this precious gift.

God had touched my life again. God was in me again. God was bringing me through again and as I began to think about the Lord in prayer and how important it all was, and the Lord begins to speak to me. I was in the bedroom praying in the Holy Ghost and the Lord said, "I want you to roll." I always wanted to go to a Pentecostal Revival when I was a teenager, but my mother said, "Oh no, those are holy-rollers." Well, I fell to my knees and then I laid out on the floor and began to roll.

I had never heard of that. I didn't know anything about it, but I laid down on my bedroom floor and I began to roll back and forth back and forth back and forth. I laid there for a while, not realizing that I was in intercession before God. At that moment, I had laid my body, my life, and my spirit down for Him. I found out that I was a Holy Roller and so very thankful for it.

During this time, I wrote to evangelists like Peter Popoff, Oral Roberts, Jimmy Swaggart, Stanley Rankin, and I received words from them that the Lord wanted to use me. The Lord also spoke to me during these prayer times to stop wearing pants, jeans, makeup, and to stop cutting my hair and after 10 years, He released me. I had proven my faithfulness because these things were not important to me anyway.

Well, my husband got the job at the coal mine, and we decided that we wanted to move to Smith Mills or Waverly, KY. However, the drive would be too far for me to travel to and from Evansville, so I quit my job at H&R Block.

My friends who knew that I prepared taxes decided to come to my house. At the time, I had a dining room table and a file box. People as far as Evansville came to my home for me to prepare their work. So, I prepared taxes during tax season in my own home and I also sold Avon, but I didn't stay with that very long because It didn't prove to be something that I really enjoyed. I wanted more of a Godly direction.

During this time in my life, I was going to the Sheep Shed to church. The Sheep Shed would bring out of town apostles and prophets along with evangelists and teachers. WOW! Was this a new direction for me? The church still needs apostles, prophets, evangelists, and teachers to come in today.

After moving to Smith Mills, I became pregnant only to miscarry my second son at 4 months. My heart was saddened, but the Lord said my son would be riding with Him when He returns. That is an awesome feeling knowing that your son is with the Master.

We got a call one day to come to the hospital, as my husband's father had taken ill, and they did not know how bad it was. Within a few days, the doctor said to call the funeral home and prepare your mother. Well, she said, "No!" because she was not ready to give him up. His daughter immediately went to the room, knowing that her father had never received Christ, and she wanted to talk to him.

He was in a semi-comma; he could hear but could not talk. She started talking to her dad and told him what the doctor said, and then she said, "Daddy you will not make it to heaven if you don't have Jesus. Follow me in prayer and I will pray, and you squeeze my hand that you understand and respond. We are taking this to God."

He nodded his head, and she continued on. When she asked him if he was ready to receive Christ, he squeezed her hand. She went into the sinner's prayer and when she finished, he squeezed her hand again. But this time it was different because he had slipped into a full comma and he was moved into another unit where he laid there for weeks. Yet, God kept him alive.

One day, my husband was sitting in the hospital room and his father woke up and said, 'Hello!" We later found out that he had an out of body spiritual experience that very few have. Jesus came and lifted him up out of his body and took him to heaven and they stood outside the gates of heaven. He said it was beautiful, and that he did not want to come back, but Jesus said you have to return and find five things to do and correct before you can enter my kingdom.

Early on I had been told that my father-in-law was mean. He had an Indian mother and when I joined the family, he and I grew to love one another very much.

Yes, he truly got saved that day, and he could not wait to get to church and testify. His daughter and I held up each of his arms while he spoke. It was awesome and very powerful. He had been set free.

After he had been released from the hospital Mr. & Mrs. Fambrough came to our home and stayed with us for two months. It was wonderful and very spiritual. He was full of the Spirit and I understood and knew that feeling very well. It is wonderful to know that he had a divine encounter and lived on for nine years. He got baptized, and at the end received the Holy Ghost and prayed in tongues, and now, he was ready to meet the master.

NEW ADVENTURE

After praying more, and spending more time to study my Bible, the Lord put Foster Care on my heart. My husband still wanted nothing to do with the church, so helping children would be a plan from the Lord. We had to apply, do some paperwork, and be interviewed. At the time I told the state that I only wanted one child. I was an only child, and I did not know if more than one child would be overwhelming or not.

Well, my first child was 6 months old, with no activity with their mother, which was fine. But shortly, and I mean shortly after, I got a call to take two brothers, ages 4 and 5 from Union County. They too had no parent communication.

For about a year I was able to put God in their lives. That alone meant everything to me because I knew that they would only be with me until their parents could regain custody. The worship was deep where we went to church and it really helped to set the boys free. When they first came their heads were hanging down and very much drawn into themselves. I put them in Head start and that was wonderful.

At their graduation from Head start, they sang a worship song from church. Let me tell you, God truly reversed inside of them, as they were more confident. That year seemed to go by fast and they moved on with their dad, only to be adopted by another family member. In the meantime, I became pregnant again, and since they were now gone, my time was spent in prayer and study, and my husband's time was spent working in the coal mine. I could not lose this next child. God blessed me and he was born, and everything was good.

The Lord began to speak to me about ministry. I was honest and said I felt that I had too much, and I would put it on a shelf and take it down when I felt the time was right. Still, in the midst of it all, I began to call and write to prophets, apostles, and other ministries and they wrote back, some even had words of prophecy and prayers.

One day when my son was very small, my husband came in from work and said, "I'm Done. I've hung It up." He was working in Henderson and decided he needed to quit. He had been in the coal mine for 8 years and that was the longest of any job he had ever had. He had some money that was put back by the company that he could draw, so I felt okay at least for the moment. Little did I know that God was moving on a lady who I had known for most of my life.

She used to babysit me when I was small, and she was married to a CPA who had taken ill. Out-of-the-blue, she called and offered me a job; in which, I was very thankful. They had the office in their home, so her husband taught me his bookkeeping accounts. They also had a lady come in every day and cook our dinner.

After I learned how to perform different duties in the office, I began to meet with and work with clients who I had never known. I knew what had to be done, so I was truly an asset. Her husband died shortly after and she and I carried on with the business. I worked there for six years, and some of the clients began to work with me on everything until the owner got remarried and moved on with her life.

CHAPTER TWO

Back Home

One day, I came home from work and my husband said he was ready for a change. We could move to Florida. I prayed about it and had peace. Even though I would leave my parents, I had family in Tampa. We drove east and west and up and down the coast to decide what looked good, and we settled in Sarasota. I got a job with the largest real estate company probably in Florida and then moved to Graybar Elec.

My oldest son got a job and his driver's permit. Things seemed to go along pretty well. But going into fall, I felt unhappy and said I wanted to go back to Kentucky. My husband was not happy at first, but then he understood. Our farm had not sold, so we had a home to go back to. As we pulled in for gas, my husband asked me to pray for a safe journey home. So, we stood in front of the gas station near the curb and prayed for God to help us. We got home 10 days before Christmas, and I got busy! I always wanted my sons to have a big Christmas, this was my way of letting them know they are loved and cared about.

After New Year's day, I began to think about my job at the tax office. I could not decide if that was the direction I should go in, but I knew that I needed to find something soon. One day, shortly after the first of the year, I received a call. It was the tax office owner's son saying, my friend and ex-employer had passed away and they wanted me to take over the business.

For the first year, I stayed in the tax office at their home because of files and the tax season was starting. After the season was over, I cleaned out all the files and moved the files into a new space inside the Citi Center Mall. It was my first time being the owner of a new office, even though I had been doing taxes for twenty years.

As I was praying one day for God to help me and always be there for me, I felt He said, "I WILL SEND," and I went into a full rest. No concerns, as I knew God had got us back to Kentucky. God is always in my heart; He was going to supply, and my needs would be met.

One day, while in my office a gentleman came in and asked for my help on getting his nonprofit status for a calling and mission he was going to open in Henderson. A rescue mission for men 18 and older who were coming from jail, homelessness, or in need. It would be a Christian home where they would be taught the Bible. It would be called Harbor House Christian Center and qualify as a Rescue Mission. When I told my dad about this man, he said to do everything you can to help him because he is the custodian at my church.

He had been in jail earlier himself and was hitchhiking to Kentucky from St. Louis. A Christian couple stopped to pick him up, and they said that they had a room prepared for him. The Lord told them that He was sending him. You are welcome to come to our home, and he went. He turned around at some point and received Jesus Christ.

After a short period of time, he returned to Kentucky where he married and began to work at the Presbyterian church. The Lord increased about taking the steps needed to bring the mission about, and he only had 35 cents in his pocket. But that didn't stop him. He started testing the waters and reaching out for help. A judge in Henderson gave him a house that needed a lot of repairs. At first, the men who came in had to go across the street to a convenience store to wash up, but they were happy to have a roof over their head and be out of the weather.

Meetings started to proceed with this need and a board of Directors had been put together. When I attended one of the meetings as a tax person, I told them I did not need to be on the board, only to be voted on by one of the ladies from the college. She said I was needed. The Lord was putting me in place. Several churches came alongside, as there was a need in Henderson County for a homeless shelter because many of our residents had been through many, many hurts and had trouble getting straight.

Joseph in the Bible, who was seventeen, with a loving father who made him a coat of many colors. Joseph had several dreams, and he shared them with his brothers. Well, they turned against him and they threw him into a pit. Sometimes family jealousy can do this. This has happened to some, even family can be hard, with no patience.

You can also slip into a pit when you are not watching where you are going. Yes, you may be in a pit, but it certainly wasn't planned. It wasn't what you needed, and you didn't see it coming.

Joseph's story is a wonderful story about being redeemed at all levels. He was left to die in that cistern. BUT GOD, BUT GOD! Genesis Chapter 37 tells his story, it is long.

Psalm says what God will do!

Psalm. 40: 1-5

40:1 *I waited patiently for the Lord and he inclined unto me and heard my cry.*

40:2 *He brought me up also out of a horrible pit, out of the miry clay, and set my feet upon a rock, and established my goings.*

40:3 *And he hath put a new song in my mouth, even praise unto our God' many shall see it, and fear, and shall trust in the Lord.*

40:4 *Blessed is the man that maketh the Lord his trust, and respecteth not the proud, nor such as turn aside to lies.*

40:5 *Many, O Lord my God, are thy wonderful works which thou has done, and thy thoughts which are to us-ward; they cannot be reckoned up in order unto thee; if I would declare and speak them, they are more than can be numbered.*

Sometimes you can jump that pit. Some have jumped straight into the pit. Sometimes you think you will take the plunge, being well aware that what you are about to do is wrong. Probably even foolish. But the escalating desire to do it exceeds the good sense not to. You had time to think, and then you did exactly what you meant to do, even if the pit turned out to be deeper and the consequences higher than you hoped.

IF YOU ARE A CONFIRMED PIT JUMPER,
YOU'VE PROBABLY GOT A PRETTY SERIOUS
LEVEL OF AUTHORITY OF THE KINGDOM.

AMEN AND AMEN

As I began to look into one of my journals, I found many prophetic words spoken over me during the time of my preparation that I want to share:

- » Brother in Christ, 6/90: You are called, so put down the fear of man.

- » One of my pastors: God does call women.

- » Pastor friend: He saw my vocal cords moving.

- » Assembly of God in Freeport, Bahamas, 6/98: God is going to use you.

- » Christian friend: 9/2000: You have been perched too long.

- » Dear Pastor, 10/19/2000: All things work together.

» (In just a few short days, he called me from the hospital, where we shared the Lord, and shortly he passed in just a day or two after leaving my office and speaking over me.

» At the funeral home, his wife said this pastor was so happy to be able to speak into my life. Even as his old life was passing, and his new life was about to begin. He also said to not fear, just put it down. Give up, God is breaking on you.)

» An Evangelist from South Africa on Mar 14,1999: Did you know you have a very deep calling in the prophetic?

» A dear sweet lady from Alabama: You will teach under much divine authority.

» Jesus sees you as being valuable. He makes us better than we are able to make ourselves. Jeremiah 29:11, 12, 13

» We are God's poetry in process, but you will be tested. If you feel you are going thru hell, don't stop there. If you hear the voice of the enemy, do not let it light in your spirit. Signs follow the believer; Believers do not have to follow signs.

As time passed, my husband decided to subdivide our farm and sell off parts of it to have money for needs. He decided to go into a trucking business, hauling air conditioners. He went into three trucking operations, only to back out after a short period of time. One of the trucking operations was hauling coal.

One day during the winter, he was delivering coal after picking it up the day before. Unbeknown to him, the coal had frozen and when he went to lift the bucket it shifted and began to turn over sideways, truck and all. My husband was inside, and he found himself sliding out of the driver's seat. As he slid out, the handle of the door sled across his hand. Thankfully, he did not go with the truck.

After trying three different trucking operations, he decided that it was time to go in for disability. He had back surgery a few years earlier, and he must have been having pain. I never knew all the problems in our home, but I ask God to be with us and help us get through. No one could bring what was needed, but God.

After thinking about it, he said we needed to get back into Henderson so I could handle my office and he would go in for disability insurance with Social Security. So, we sold what was left of the farm and bought the nicest home I had ever had. A tri-level on an acre of land. We had plenty of room and my mother and aunt helped us with kitchen appliances and dining room furniture.

At this time, I also purchased a ladies clothing store from one of my clients. I had been her bookkeeper for several years. I was able to give my mother a job since my father had passed and she no longer had his retirement. I operated it for ten years, but when Goody's came in, it made the business go down. That is when I decided to make the building a tax office. The parking was better, and the business held.

After a few years, a wonderful man came alongside and donated a corner lot for a new building. Everything began to fall in place, and donations started for Harbor House. We made a loan at the bank for part of it, but it was short-lived. We were able to house 16 men, beds, cabinets, and furniture began to come in. We had a room toward the front that was to be used for a chapel. So we started meetings there. It was able to seat a large group. After a while, we were donated $10,000.00 to put toward starting a women's shelter. It was enough to purchase a mobile home that could house four women.

WORDS GIVEN TO ME

I remember a word from a prophet, earlier in time. He said *"For Yea, my daughter, keep your eyes upon my word and your ears tuned to My good. Keep your spirit alert and listen and you will hear. Look and you will see...reach out and you will find. Even now I the Lord your God have ordained that miracles are about to be released upon thee."*

Satan wants you to park by your problem, but I say unto thee, *"This day arise and move in faith and I shall open the door for thee, and you shall walk into my complete victory, harmony, health, peace, and prosperity. I am the finisher of your faith. Do not look at your problems, but look to me, for I am the solution to every problem in your life. I am the way, the truth that you have looked for, and source of all life."*

{44}

LET YOUR
HOLY FIRE FALL

During this same time, I heard of a revival in Pensacola, Fla. Being held at Brownsville Assembly of God. I had moved already to Henderson, so I started going to the Assembly of God Church in Henderson. On Father's day in 1995, the Holy Spirit had fallen in Pensacola, and God blessed them with a divine visitation.

Word was getting out about the revival, and my church had pulled together a group with three vans of people to go. I knew I would be on that list. Actually, I was the first to register for the trip. It was a good group, everyone wanted more, and we all helped one another to be in one accord. Lines of people formed every day early in the morning so they would be guaranteed a seat when the doors opened in the evening.

One of the girls, who is a dear friend, had already been to the revival and she told me to follow her to the front. The worship was heavy and very anointed, and there were people standing across the front of the church. As we stood there a young man stepped off the platform and came up to me. He laid his hand on my forehead and said, "LORD OPEN UP THE WINDOWS OF HEAVEN FOR MY SISTER." I fell back immediately onto the carpeted floor. I was laying on my back when my feet began to shake back and forth from right to left.

As it started with my feet, it began to move up to my ankles, calf, and thighs, rotating very hard. My mind kicked in and I began to question myself saying, "What are people around me going to think?" It had already reached my waist as I was thinking about what people thought. It was starting to slow down and maybe was going to stop. I knew that was the wrong way to think, and while I was thinking, I began to say to my God "I do not care what people think, I have come for God's visit, and I trust You with my life. I give him everything."

Dear Heavenly Father,

I come in the name of Jehovah

I ask that the Spirit of love begin to do a work in this Body of Believers. Love for others, inside and outside of their walls. This is the season you are being called to be a people of God to be taken into the higher places. Feel the shift, and begin to shape yourself into a new realm where it begins to change your culture. Changing your culture back to the way that it was when you where a New Beginning when your founding was set at record. Back to the Kingdom realm where there are no walls that divide, but reach out to others and thereby changing the atmosphere wherever you are, with more love for Jesus.

This Body of Believers and property, I dedicate to the Lord and ask that it return to the former days, when it first began and had a zeal for the Lord and much was done to advance the Kingdom. I say come forth in Jesus name. Come out of alignment with anything that does not agree with the word of God. Bring new clarity, power, unity and restablish the love to go deeper. Let them realize that they have been redeemed from the curse of the law, and allow the mysteries and wonders of the Lord to come forth in this body. Return to the God of their childhood and their founding fathers. And as in Revelations, I say that you will not loose your lampstand and be not removed but reclaim your land, and work for the Lord and take back any thing that has been stolen from you.

Just as in Psalms, Lift up your heads O ye gates, and be ye lifted up, ye everlasting doors and the King of Glory shall come in. Who is this King of Glory, the Lord strong and mighty, the Lord mighty in battle. Father I ask for a new release of your Kingdom here in this place. A release of God that will take this body and go beyond whatever it might ask or think. Take this body to the place of hearing and seeing what thus sayeth the Lord. I ask that the blinders be removed, so that the Glorious sunlight Of the Lord can come and deliver those things from darkness. I ask that the gifts, talents, and skills, be released with increased anointing. Create this body anew for your pleasure. Give them Godly creativity and bring the personality of this group into alignment with your divine will and plan. God, we ask that you water this body with a refreshing as in the book of Ezekiel, and we ask that the water release a flood. I ask that the river of God begin to flow through their altar and flow through these people and flow out of their four walls into the highway and byways and care for the homeless, down and out, and the unlovable and the lost. This is the Day of the Lord, a time that we are to return to our first love.

I ask that the people of this Body, be in subjection to the governing authorities. God is the ultimate authority and we desire to establish Gods government here in this city. Come out and take the seven mountains with your sphere of influence. Release a new sound in this place. Come into your true identity, becoming Christlike. Let this church no longer have business as usual. I ask that the Lord impart a new place, and a new design, to live, move and have their being in Christ. I ask Lord, that these people be

{47}

found faithful, and righteous, so that the passion and dream of a Mighty God can do His work in their midst.

May worship and praise rise from this place. May this house be transformed by the renewing of its mind so that it will not be conformed to this world. Allow God to transform this place, and be a light and not a judge. Allow God to change us so we can transform ourselves so that our environment will change.

As it says in Isaiah 55: So shall your word go forth out of my mouth and it will not return void, but it will accomplish that which you please and it shall go out with joy and be lead forth with peace, as we link arms together as one. As we sprinkle salt on your grounds I know that purity and cleansing will take place. Cleanse their thinking where there has been division, addiction, graven images and idols of any sort be now null and void and let the integrating work of the Holy Spirit come and fill believers. We need to view and live life from the center of our Spirit union with the Holy Spirit and not in compartments where some have been separated from His power and influence. So Father, integrate them by the power of the Holy Spirit and the truth of your word. I ask that this prayer be a battering ram and battle axe into the atmosphere and every crack and crevice. In Jesus name, I ask that the hidden treasure be found, loosed, unshackled, and brought forth by the power that is within this group of believers. Say yes to freedom, and no to bondage. Jesus bring this place back to its sure foundation that the people can possess the land, and send forth wealth to be able to do the works of God. RELEASE KINGDOM ACTIVITY   IN JESUS NAME

Even the calling He gave me 20 years ago; I repent that it took so long for me to arrive. But the Lord must be speaking because I never knew He could move your body as He did. And for three days, I received deliverance, Fire, and power. It was such an experience to be laying on the floor next to someone from a foreign country who had a box with an interpreter. But we were all in the same Spirit.

The Joy of the Lord truly became my strength. I have never laid out on the floor so much in all my spiritual life. We were there for three days and everyone received something. As we were loading up for the trip home, I began to think about taking down some notes of things that I had received. I was so full. Then the Lord began to speak to me. As I laid my head back, I was fully-filled with

His presence. He began to speak. *"FOR TRULY YOU HAVE BEEN THROUGH THE FIRE, BUT NOW YOU HAVE BEEN FILLED WITH MY FIRE. YOU HAVE WADED OUT INTO THE DEEP, AND NOW YOU CAN WADE ON OUT INTO THE DEEPER WATER. YOU CAN LIFT YOUR FEET AND FLOAT ON, FOR I AM TAKING CARE OF EVERYTHING. AND YOU CAN DANCE IT IN."*

WELLLLLLLLLLLLLLLLLLLLLLLL, THERE WAS A TOTAL REST AND RELEASE WITHIN MY LIFE. I AM NOT PERFECT, BUT I SERVE THE ONE THAT IS.

CHAPTER THREE

CALLED TO MINISTRY

The next time to be in service at church brought me even closer to Him. I began to meditate on the events at Brownsville, while sitting on my pew I felt to rise up during worship, and praise Him for what He had done. I fell out in the Spirit, and He began to speak to me again and said, "Arise and shine for thy light is come and the glory of the Lord is risen upon thee."

Then several scriptures started coming to me. Everything that had ever been spoken over me for His will was coming to fruition. The Lord said, "Even the things that had been spoken against you have been shaken off."

Isaiah 59:21,

"As for me, this is my covenant with them, saith the Lord. My Spirit that is upon thee, and my words which I have put in thy mouth, shall not depart out of thy mouth., nor out of the mouth of thy seed, nor out of the mouth of thy seed's seed, saith the Lord, from henceforth and forever."

Isaiah 61:1, 2, 6

"The Spirit of the Lord is upon me because the Lord hath anointed me to preach good tidings unto the meek; he hath sent me to bind up the brokenhearted, to proclaim liberty to the captives, and the opening of the prison to them that are bound.

2 To proclaim the acceptable year of the Lord, and the day of vengeance of our God, to comfort all that mourn:

3 To appoint unto them at mourn in Zion, to give unto them beauty for ashes, the oil of joy for mourning, the garment of praise for the spirit of heaviness: that they might be called trees of righteousness, the planting of the Lord, that he might be glorified.

6 But ye shall be named the Priests of the Lord, men shall call you the ministers of our God, ye shall eat the riches of the gentiles, and in their glory shall ye boast yourselves."

After this visitation, I was ready to go into a deeper place when the Holy Ghost was introduced to me, but that was only the beginning. I found that I had to be a seeker. The word says "Seek ye first the Kingdom of God and His righteousness and all these things will be added unto you."

During this time, the Lord also said, "IT IS TIME." while I was on the floor. My heart was stirring, and I began to think of Jesus and what would He want for me, and what kind of obstacles would there be for me. I felt it was time for me to take my position to seek Jesus in a deeper way. I knew that nothing would stop me as I had been spoken to by God, Himself.

I had to go through some testing and equipping before I could truly come into position, and of course, I found that at Brownsville Revival. The thoughts of being used by God seemed to have been drying up was totally watered by the River. Nothing would go wrong; yet, I had everything to gain. I gave my husband to God a long time ago and he was no longer my responsibility. I had done everything I could.

I brought some videos from services at the revival. I did not know what they were but knew that I would enjoy them. One evening, I asked my husband if we could watch one of the services and he said, yes. It was Steve

Hill; he was precious but has now gone on to be with Jesus.

As the message started after the worship service, Steve Hill stepped down off the platform. He was walking up the aisle, even toward the camera that was filming this message. He looked square into the camera and pointed his finger into the camera and said, "Sir, the one who is sitting in a red recliner there at home. It is time for you to come in. Don't hesitate! Today is the day of salvation. You cannot wait any longer."

As I was sitting behind him on the couch, I began to realize that my husband was sitting in a red recliner. I almost bit my tongue knowing that the Lord was speaking to him. The message went on as we sat, and nothing was said. I had already talked so much over the years and tried to live by example, and I had just given up with talk.

As the message went on, it was wonderful. Then Steve turned again toward the camera, pointed his finger, and began to speak to the man in the red recliner again, "It is time he began to say." At that moment, my husband began to get up and I said to myself, well, he is leaving the room. But no, that is not what he did; instead, he fell out on the floor and began to cry. I had never seen this out of him, but the Lord had spoken, and I left Him alone to be able to take in what happened. It was a divine visitation and we had two years of peace and tranquility.

A few days later, while watching TV in the evening, my husband asked me to pray for him. He wanted me to lay hands on his eyes. He had been told that the arteries behind his eyes were like silver threads by two doctors from Vanderbilt in Nashville, and this is a hardening that can happen. As I laid my hands on his eyes, I did not feel anything, I just prayed and left it at that. Not realizing that in just a few weeks he had a local appointment with an eye doctor.

As the doctor began to examine, I began to ask the doctor about what he saw, only to have my husband cut in and say, "Dr. she's wanting to know about the silver threads behind the eyes." The doctor said, "No, the arteries are not silver threads, but they are very healthy." As we left the office and got in the car, my husband said, "You know who done that don't you?" and I said, yes. Never receiving a thank you or anything, I thanked the Lord for His touch: still, my husband still did not want to go to church.

The next Sunday as I went to early prayer and worship class, I was there with several others to pray. As they began to pray, I felt to pull aside and hear from the Master. He said, "I want you to intercede for nations." I immediately went to my knees and began to intercede and some of the class did not understand. Yet, the Lord was leading me into an intercession class that He wanted.

My pastor approved and I began to organize a class. There were about six of us. We may have not been many, but we were mighty. I got a world map, as well as a list of the local prayer needs of our community. We would pray and the Lord would give words and direction, and they were all special.

As time went on, our morning prayer and worship on Sunday carried on. One of the ladies who came to be with us each Sunday came in with her arms bandaged up. She had something that broke out all over her two arms. As we began to pray, the Lord said, "Go out and get the bucket in your car and fill in with water. When you pray for her, lay her arms in the water." So, I went and got the water.

As we gathered for prayer, she removed her bandages and laid her arms into the bucket, and we all prayed in agreement. We did not see anything at that time, but the Lord healed her after several days. That bucket is special to me today, even though it has been 20 plus years.

This was teaching me that we do have divine appointments. The Lord said to me, "To begin to renew my mind even more, as everything around me was going to accelerate. I was coming into a new era." Well, I found that I had faith that must increase. Also, I was totally believing that we have to think, pray, ask for more power, miracles, and more of His plan. I believe God's plans are there to fulfill, if we will keep walking. I have no clue what others have to go through, but Jesus truly does.

As I look back on my spiritual life and childhood, I would be so thankful. As I returned to my normal working life, I never let go of God. I had to go into another office room one day at work and get on the floor. The Spirit was so heavy that I had to get on the floor. I just humbled myself and what I call "soaked" in His presence. It was like governmental authority was being imparted to me. And yes, the kingdoms of this earth are also the kingdoms of our God.

I came into the calling of a tax person and how I would have to question everyone and be very serious about who's return I was preparing; their citizenship and other important papers. I had a gentleman come in the office one time and I had to check his citizenship, green card, and other forms of ID. I felt that he would never be back to my office but when it was all said and done, he said, "Wow, you do check your clients?" And I said, "YES!" He is coming even today; I made a friend and client for many years.

I remember the times that I would hear "Believe it and Receive it!" A possible potential, not just existing, but having an expectant attitude. I have found that the most powerful words in the English language are the ones you chose to say to yourself. Our internal dialogue has profound effects on our potential to achieve happiness and success.

There are people who come from horrible beginnings, who've learned how to talk themselves into successful living. If we choose to focus on what's possible and talk to ourselves about what success will look like and feel like, good things follow; especially, when you speak to yourself in hymns, psalms, and spiritual songs. Have you ever said to yourself?

I want to be whole.
I want to be prosperous.
I want faith and hope in my life.
I want to be healed. IN JESUS NAME!
I do not want to be a wound addict.
I want to look at life differently.
I do not want to use my emotional wounds as an excuse.
I want to rise up and take charge.
I want to know the truth, as it is the power unto salvation.

F - FALSE
E - EVIDENCE
A - APPEARING
R - REAL

I have heard this several times, and I am very thankful that FEAR has no place in me. I preach, that if you will allow God room, He will lift you up to your highest when you are at your lowest. No governmental mountain or economy can come against the expansion God wants to do in the earth. AND WHAT HE WANTS TO DO IN YOU!

So many people speak and confess the wrong things. Faith-filled words will put you over and Fear filled words will defeat you.

Mark 11:22, 23, 24

²² *"And Jesus answering saith unto them HAVE FAITH IN GOD.*

²³ *For verily I say unto you, that whosoever shall say unto this mountain, Be thou removed, and be thou cast into the sea; and shall not doubt in his heart but shall believe that those things which he saith shall come to pass, he shall have whatsoever he saith.*

²⁴ *Therefore I say unto you, What things soever ye desire, when ye pray, believe that ye receive them, and ye shall have them."*

GOD HAS LAW. IT IS SPIRITUAL LAW THAT TRANSCENDS TO THE EARTH REALM.

- » Do you have Jesus?
- » What are you doing with him?
- » Does He go shopping, to school, or to work with you?
- » Do you pack your life in your own hands, instead of lifting your life to God?

DOUBT SEES THE OBSTACLES; FAITH SEES THE WAY

DOUBT SEES THE DARKEST NIGHT; FAITH SEES THE DAY

DOUBT DREADS TO TAKE A STEP; FAITH SOARS ON HIGH

DOUBT QUESTIONS "WHO BELIEVES?" FAITH ANSWERS "I"

FAITH WILL BE FEARLESS

FAITH WILL BE OUR PROTECTION

FAITH WILL BE OUR PRESERVATION

FAITH WILL DELIVER US

FAITH WILL BRING US VICTORY

FAITH WILL TRIUMPH IN US

FAITH WILL BRING US PHYSICAL STRENGTH

FAITH WILL FEED US

FAITH WILL BRING US BOLDNESS

FAITH WILL UTTER RELIANCE

FAITH WILL GIVE INTEGRITY

FAITH WILL BRING US THE PROMISE

FAITH WILL BRING US ENDURANCE

FAITH WILL CONQUER TEMPTATIONS

FAITH WILL HELP US BUILD

FAITH WILL BREAK THE CHAINS OF BONDAGE TO YOUR MIND, YOUR WILL, AND YOUR SOUL.

My brother in Christ, who has now gone to be with Jesus, shared about His Glory and that God has called us to be carriers of His Glory and presence. God's glory, His splendor, Honor, and Power came to change us to make us like Him. His glory can become so great in our lives that we will be people who sense his presence, and He can take over our lives, and we can be FULL, FULL, FULL.

He wants us to take His Glory to the world. He wants us to overflow (The degree to which you allow His presence to overflow in you is the degree to which the presence can flow out from you). We are containers, and He wants to demonstrate His Spirit and Power to the world, and He will do that through you and me.

As containers of His Presence, we are also carriers of His Glory. YES, AMEN!

As time was moving on toward Christmas, I began to get my office ready for another tax season. I was so blessed to be able to hire several employees who would learn and possibly grow with me. My company was growing, and it was a joy.

One day, within three months of my revival experience, I received a call from a lady in Kentucky who was an officer with Kentucky Aglow International. She wanted to know if I would be interested in becoming Henderson County's first president and begin the ministry to women in this county.

I knew then that the Lord was going to expand my territory, and that I would accept whatever came my way. I would do my best to fulfill it and be that vessel unto honor. My name had been turned in by a lady from Chicago who was also a leader of Aglow and was there to help my foster son. We had been reunited, and she and her husband had come to meet me.

My oldest son was about to be married, so they all came to be with us. My foster sons and my oldest natural son had grown close during their time in our home. God had done a wonderful work in their lives. The oldest foster son had accelerated in his music career and been employed at the largest gospel station in Chicago. He also was sent to the Dove Awards in Nashville to receive his highest award for his service well done and I got to attend. What a joy! WOW! WOW! WOW!

OTHER WORDS GIVEN TO ME

Evangelist, 10/97: Sister you are going to go thru a holy visitation (From Brownsville)

(WHAT HE DID NOT KNOW WAS THAT I WAS RIGHT IN THE MIDDLE OF THAT VISIT).

» Lady Prophetess, 6/98: The Deborah anointing has been given unto thee.

» Lady at church in Evansville, Indiana in 1998: Said she saw a ring of fire all around me.

» Lady from First Assembly in 12/98: Your heart is blazing with fire.

I remember being spoken to by another prophet that I would have a ministry as unto the Lord. I learned not to judge people who did not have money from my mother. She always said, do not talk about anyone until you have walked in their moccasins.

My mother could talk to anyone and have a caring heart, and across the years she served as well. Her church had different areas that she and my father carried with other members. During that time, she had slight cancer and overcame it. One day, she met a gentleman who spoke a prayer over her, and she has spoken this prayer over her children at home during times of get-togethers. It is like this:

I SAID A PRAYER FOR YOU TODAY

AND KNOW GOD MUST HAVE HEARD

I FELT THE ANSWER IN MY HEART

ALTHOUGH HE SPOKE NOT A WORD

I DIDN'T ASK FOR WEALTH OR FAME

I KNEW YOU WOULDN'T MIND

I ASKED HIM TO SEND TREASURES

OF A FAR MORE LASTING KIND

I PRAYED THAT HE WOULD BE NEAR YOU

AT THE START OF EACH NEW DAY

TO GRANT YOU HEALTH AND BLESSINGS

AND FRIENDS TO SHARE YOUR WAY

I ASKED FOR HAPPINESS FOR YOU

IN ALL THINGS GREAT AND SMALL
BUT IT WAS FOR HIS LOVING CARE
I PRAYED THE MOST OF ALL.
WITH LOVE WILLIE ANN, GRANDMOTHER.
THIS PRAYER WAS WRITTEN BY CATHOLIC
COMPANY

At this time, I still served the Harbor House Christian Center. I had been given a word about this calling earlier as well. A pastor friend had told me that I was called to put down the fear of man. God calls who He wants and prepares the way.

When I thought about an international ministry, it really exhilarated my energy and faith. I knew that this was the Lord and that I could do this. God did a suddenly in my life, revealing to me that His love was a love of another kind, and not earthly. He knew I could do this.

The Lord brought four other women alongside with a heart and calling much like mine. Ladies from church that I knew and trusted to stand with me. I served seven years and I saw many women who had their standard of living raised to a new level. I was also opened up to a new level of power and anointing from God.

I got to travel to conferences in and out of state. They were always powerful, and we always received them. God was with us. My first luncheon was called "Restoring

Spiritual Integrity" and the Kentucky prayer director spoke. She was a precious person and truly had the heart of God.

I found out that God is not calling an audience, He is calling an army. We are not in the dead sea but in the flowing river and I had stepped out into that river, and He was continuing to carry me. Jesus sees us as being valuable and He makes us better than we are able to make ourselves. If you have a plan given by God, He will be with you to bring it to fruition. If we have a mess, make it a message and turn your test into a testimony.

Was I really ready to look ahead and not look back? Does the Lord really have all things worked out for me? Maybe it was time to look ahead with some God thoughts because most of the world is thinking about self-thoughts. God must love me a lot to bring me into all of the things I see in front of me. The word of God is a treasure. Never give up, give out, or give in, and with Jesus all things are possible. He is my fortress and I have found that His thoughts get His actions.

I would always pray before the meetings for the Lord to position us to receive what He has for us. We always wanted to encounter God's presence, which triggers his power; that Jesus would break every struggle, fear, doubt, and discord, knowing that the truth will set us free.

This was in 1998, and it came to me so quickly after my revival experience. I was so thankful that the Lord was allowing me to be a part of what He was doing in the earth. It seemed to be a new day, and many things were changing in the spiritual realm. A new day, a new song, and a new excitement in the earth, or maybe it was just in me. There are times in all of our lives that He has to carry us, and He wants us to know that He is strong and loves us and is happy that we need His strength to be carried by Him.

During the conferences, many new directions and anointings were given. One of the most special was the conference shared about Deborah's life. At the end they prayed for the Deborah anointing to be upon us. As I prayed about it and began to allow it to soak into my heart, I realized that I had some Deborah in me.

First, I was government-friendly. I could seek and search what was needed by clients and those who needed direction according to the law, the Natural and Spiritual law. And then the part of going with Barak into battle. Barak would not go without her. And as I look back, many times I have been thanked by the founder of Harbor House for my service. For standing with him, supporting him, and putting my time toward his calling. It was always to help others.

Deborah was also a prophetess. Tongues and interpretation came on me stronger in the 1990s. The Lord has given me tongues and interpretation many many times. I have interpreted even at Assembly of God statewide meetings. The Lord has given me poems, and prayers over the years also. I have a palm tree at my office to remind me of Deborah. To continually let me know that I can do all things, IN THE NAME OF JESUS. I feel my life is parallel with hers. She was married, but you hear very little about her husband.

I wanted to continue to do what I could for the homeless here in Henderson. He cares about women, and even at the time, a way was being made for a trailer that could house 4 women. One of the ladies that I used in the Aglow ministry lived within the block, and she became the overseer of the home. It worked well. I had Aglow meetings at the home for women. I have found that when you follow, He will lead, and also multiply.

I always let the ladies know in Aglow to be thankful to the Lord for He had allowed us to see and be a part of what He was doing in the earth. It was a New Day, New Song, and a New Excitement in the earth during this time. In Aglow, we were brought into another level of ministers and ministry. The Lord allowed us to see and hear what was coming forth on several levels.

There are times in our lives that He has to carry us, and He wants us to know always that His strength is of another kind. I totally believe that the church of Jesus Christ was seeing a shift. I know that for myself, I was now overseeing two groups. Aglow ladies and the Harbor House ladies.

I began to receive other prophetic words. I looked into my journal and these were given from Aglow International:

» Aglow Head Director of Kentucky, 9/99: You are a warrior, your amour is worn, and tarnished. Start shining your amour.

» Aglow, KY President, 10/98: The mantle of the Lord is upon you.

» Aglow Prayer Leader, 9/99: You are a prism, with light shining out of all directions

He had put His big arms of love around me and let me know that He was equipping me for service. He had taken all the doubt, fear, and anxiousness totally away, and brought me into a freedom not many people get to enjoy. One day in 2001, I went to my tax office and as I entered the building the Lord said, "Get your papers" Well, I had to chuckle. There are papers everywhere. So I asked, "What papers do you mean, as there are papers all over the place here?" And He answered, "Ministry papers"

So I went to my pastor. He was from New York and he was very supportive of me and believed in me. We called Springfield, MO Assembly of God main office to get my course of study with Global University and he would write a letter of reference. I was slow getting this started.

I still had to pinch myself occasionally because I could see that He was bringing me to another level and another place of fruition. I had been faithful, and He must have been watching me. So I told the Lord that if I could get through the first three studies I would continue on and complete the total of eleven. Then I would truly know that I was on the path that the Lord had laid out for me.

He was opening a door that no man could shut. I could make it, and it was time to share it with my family. Everyone was supportive, and the Lord had already revealed it to my husband. He told me he already knew I was called. He was supportive but still did not want to go to church.

One day, I came home from work and had forgotten to place a very important call to one of my clients. I always follow up on what is needed. Well, I drove up the driveway and got out in a hurry.

As I started up the sidewalk to go to my back door in a hurry, I realized that I had walked up on a large snake on the sidewalk. I did not even realize it until I stopped and looked down. It was a large snake, and it raised its head to look at me right in the eyes as I looked down at him. I stood within one foot of the snake's head, and we were eye to eye. I said to myself, I cannot suffer this thing to live and walked over for a hoe to cut its head off and turned around to only see no snake. I looked under the bushes and shrubs everywhere only to find nothing.

The Lord Said, "IF YOU WILL KEEP THE CONNECTION AND CONCENTRATION ON ME JUST AS THAT PHONE CALL, YOU WILL TREAD UPON SERPENTS."

The snake had totally disappeared, very fast. Ha Ha, he must have been afraid of me. My husband killed the snake the next day, as it came back into my yard. So he got his.

One afternoon, as I was preparing supper, my youngest son came in. My husband was sitting at the dining room table. We were all saying, hello, when my husband began to cry. Well, it was shocking in a way, as I had only seen this one time and my son had never seen it. My son went over to his dad and put his arm on his shoulder. My son then turned and went downstairs. I followed him down, as my husband came down also. I told my son "Well you have never thought you would ever see this happen, did you?"

My husband stepped down to us and put his arms around our necks, as to hug us. Then he said, "She's cleaned house." Well, To this day I do not know what he meant, but a clean house means some changes were made. The Holy Ghost swept thru our home during that time at revival. Thank you, Jesus. It just did not last.

I began to get my mind back on my studies. It was slow, but it began to come together. Our Kentucky Head Administrator came to church for a special meeting. We had already met earlier, and I began to tell him about what was ahead for me. He was very pleased and knew that I was called, and he would be there for me in the future.

I had to do the study along with my tax office workload. So, I was very slow about finishing, but finally, I did finish. We now had another pastor at my church. He was very caring and supportive, as he had been going to this church for many years. It was so wonderful to be excepted by pastors, men, and women alike. As I had been told that women were not called and that was another's doctrine, thank God it is not the Lords.

I finished the certified/credentialed level in 2006, and I was invited to attend the cap and gown service where I would graduate in Springfield, MO. My husband took me to the service where 600 graduated but only 27 were able to attend, and all the other graduates were from other nations.

This was such a humbling experience to be numbered among others from all over the world with the same mission, and I saw God was moving all over the globe. There were several women just like me, and even about the same age who was getting their diplomas, I felt so much of a part of something so much greater than myself.

In October 2006, after graduating I was asked to do Sunday morning services at the Harbor House Rescue Mission. I had already been a founding director and stayed with the ministry for many years. Actually, since 1988. I said, " I would pray about it." A few days later, and after much prayer I felt the Lord say, "I want to come, but there is no one there on Sundays." That was all I needed, as Jesus had rescued me out of all concerns, and I knew He wanted to rescue others.

Assemblies of God are truly out to rescue America, and I have begun in Henderson County. The services were open to the public and even the residents of the mission had their families come. They did respond very well, even my husband started to come to church on Sundays for the first time. That was truly a God thing. You might call it a miracle. I found out that I was speaking to him also during the messages.

I did everything I could to bring these gentlemen into the reality of a living God. Who would be true and honest with them? That you have to turn everything over to Him. This is the only one who can turn your past into pearls, struggles into strategies, future into focus, and tragedies into triumphs!

Eight Key Ideas: BELIEVE, TRUST, AND OBEY, SUBMISSION, FORGET THE PAST, FOCUS, CHOICE, THANKFULNESS, AND PURPOSE/DETERMINED.

The victory is settled, and you can reject what distracts you. Think and recount your past victories. Specialize in your talents and be strong with who you are and who He made you to be.

1 COR 15:10

"But by the grace of God I am what I am and his grace which is bestowed upon me was not in vain; but I laboured more abundantly than they all; yet not I, but the grace of God which was with me."

One of my Aglow ministry ladies and her husband came alongside and did music and singing, which was such a blessing. Then in 2007, I was invited to attend the

73rd Annual Kentucky District Council conference in Louisville, where I would attend the Ordination service and be recognized as a credentialed/certified minister. It was a time like no other. My husband, my sons, who were both now married, along with my daughter-in-law and one grandchild who had been born. My mother was also with us and it was such a blessing for us all to be together.

At this time, I resigned from Aglow, as I wanted to see about the homeless and give more time to my Sunday morning services. I had enjoyed everything, and we had discontinued the women's home, as Henderson was moving forward with homeless help. We now have several homes for those in need in Henderson County because they followed the Harbor Houses example.

CHAPTER FOUR

DEEPER WATER

As I returned from the service in Louisville, I was thinking about where I was at. A credentialed minister with Assemblies of God, and a Pastor of a rescue mission. I had to pinch myself again. I was so humbled and satisfied, and thankful that I was able to share with my father, who had gone on to be with Jesus, that the Lord was going to use me.

I prayed with my dad one day on our knees, and he renewed his salvation. It was wonderful. That day has never come with my husband at that time, but I kept on moving. One thing my husband did do, he thanked me for all the work I did for him with the trucking companies. The bookkeeping and all that was involved. That was so kind.

I do not feel to leave my tax office during this time. Yet, I want to encourage women who feel they are called; God will make a way. Some husbands will not allow spiritual growth in their wives. Which is wrong. Women grow spiritually and follow Jesus just like men.

My husband's mother was a Godly woman who had rules: prayer, no cussing, and a strong bible reader. My husband told me after we married that he thought I had money. Well, I did not have money, but I had something more important...**A CALLING.**

I thank the Lord that he now attends my services at the shelter. I didn't even have to ask him to come. He just showed up one day after I started. That is a miracle. God does increase your territory. I have now been allowed to represent God's business, as I have done what He asked. I want to walk so close, that He can whisper, and I will hear Him.

During this time, I inherited a farm. A friend and I took care of one of my clients and she left everything she had to us. The Lord had already told me that He was taking care of everything, so I rested. I was able to take care of all debts and become debt-free. I even gave my husband $10,000 and a truck. I was able to tithe, help my sons, and all the Lord told me to do. Yes, I have been faithful.

During Christmas Eve 2007, at our Christmas dinner with our children, things seemed unsettled as my husband was saying things off the wall that I did not understand. Yet, we opened our gifts and continued to spend our time together. My two sons had gotten their dad a toolbox, but it was inside of the garage. So, they asked their dad to go out with them to the garage.

As they were going thru the room which leads to the garage, my husband got up in my youngest son's face and then my oldest son's face. He spued out horrible profanity, but my sons held it together, probably because of fear, but I am sure they were glad to leave that day. I feel it was the church and money, and that he could no longer handle it. He wanted control and that probably meant, leaving God out.

I knew he had crossed over into another place. A place I had not seen before. Yes, he could be ugly to you, but this was another place. One day, I asked the Lord what do I do? He said, "Either talk or you can walk." So, I waited for a few days. My husband asked us to forgive him, but it was like getting a snack at McDonald's, "I'm sorry, but let's get a coke." Not really caring about what he had done, nor was it was heartfelt. So, his apology got us nowhere.

Each day I would see if I had a leading, and after a week, I finally told him that we had to talk.

He replied, "There was nothing wrong with me, I am OK mentally and physically, and then he said, "I am going downstairs to watch TV."

I said to the Lord, "You heard what he said."

The Lord responded, "What have I told you? Talk or walk."

So I went to my bedroom with a sack and gathered a few belongings. Afterward, I made my way to the basement, and said, "Well, I am gone."

My husband replied, "Where are you going, to your mothers?"

I said, "I don't really know."

I went to my youngest son's house and he helped me get into a Holiday Inn. That night I called every prayer line I knew about and the next day I went to my mother's house because her door would never be closed to me.

Shortly after, it was New Year's Day, and yes, it would be a New Year for me as well. My Father does not want me to live in abuse and ugliness. My husband was ugly to us over the years, so I prayed much about my children and the actions of their father. Compared to the world today, I guess I can say we made it.

Yes, I am sure my children had to endure many things, but I know the Lord is with my sons and I know He leads and guides them, and that is what's important. They both have had visitations and they have heard the Word all of their lives and the Word lives in them. Now, that is what's important to all of us because they know who to turn to in the time of need.

So, after moving in with my mother, I kept on going to the Harbor House for Sunday services and it was wonderful working toward recovery for those who needed it. The Lord brought many to the altar, and I was able to baptize thirty of them. Included with that number were my youngest son and his wife, who came one day to also be baptized. My oldest son came along with his family and his guitar, so we worshiped.

What a joy!!!!!!!!!!

During this time, my children and I also attended the Presbyterian Church where my mother was given the highest award of receiving the Honorary Life Membership Award. It is given to recognize outstanding commitment to Christ and the mission of the church. Her pin received stands for personal and corporate response to Jesus Christ as we nurture our faith, it also indicates our work for peace in our lives and throughout the world, and to know that our sins are forgiven, and we are free to live in Christ who is at the center of our lives.

Well, the new year had begun, so I pondered on the Lord and His goodness and what laid ahead. One day, as I was preparing to go to work, I got in my car and the Lord began to speak. As I thought about what was going on, I realized He was giving me a poem, and He said,

NEVER BE AFRAID TO GO FORWARD

NEVER BE AFRAID TO BE CALLED MY OWN

I ONLY WANT WHAT IS GOOD AND TRUE

AND I WILL FULFILL MY WILL IN YOU

I NEVER MAKE MISTAKES

YOUR HEART IS PURE AND YOUR LOVE IS TRUE

I AM WITH YOU IN WHATEVER YOU DO

I AM YOUR STRENGTH

I AM YOUR COURAGE

I AM TOUCHING YOUR LIFE IN A NEW WAY

YOU ARE MY CHILD, AND I HAVE CHOSEN YOU

I KNOW YOU ARE TRUE AND I CAN COUNT ON YOU

DO NOT BE AFRAID, MY LOVE SURROUNDS

I WILL CARRY YOU WHEN THINGS SEEM DOWN

SO LIFT YOUR HEAD AND CARRY ON,

FOR MY STRONG ARM IS ONE YOU CAN LEAN ON

GIVEN TO LINDA ON 2/2008

As I think about my life now and the different things that changed. My husband would no longer be in my services at the mission, and I would be more available for my mother. As I continued on with Sunday services, I brought many things to stir up the atmosphere. I spoke prophetic words to those when the Lord would lead during the morning. At the end of one service, I was approached by a middle to older age gentleman, and he knelt down in front of me. He did not say much, but he blessed me and honored me for my message.

I totally believe he was a present-day disciple, apostle, prophet, and everything else. His countenance was strong, and he may have been an angel. He said he would be there for three days and then he would be moving on. I was so blessed because God was on the scene. One day, the Lord said, *"I WANT YOU TO GO TO EVERY CHURCH IN THIS COUNTY AND STAND ON THEIR GROUND, SPRINKLE SALT AND PRAY THE PRAYER THAT I WILL GIVE YOU"*

I began to be silent so that I could receive the prayer. No, It did not come overnight. In fact, it took about a week to put it together. I began what the Lord instructed me to do, and it took a while. I drove all over the county delivering the message because I am believing that every church in this county will fulfill her destiny.

As I thought about my future and what would happen with my marriage, I often wondered about how it would play out, but I just kept on living my daily life, happy and knowing that it was in God's hands. There was no communication with my husband, and then late in 2008, he filed for divorce. I could not see a way for this to recover, so I started seeing a lawyer. Some friends of mine ask me how I was able to live with this man? They said it seemed like I felt better and was more relaxed.

When the divorce was over, I was thinking about my ministry papers and everything I worked for would be taken away. So after the start of 2009, I contacted the head superintendent of KY Assemblies of God. My husband and I had been in his office in 2006 for prayer and this is where the Lord led us. That was amazing at that time, having my husband there with me. I did not know at that time that he was unhappy.

All those times he stood with me during my schooling and graduation and then going on to Harbor House; yet he was not ready to go forward but come to a complete stop. After speaking with the head office and superintendent, I was thrilled to be informed that the rules for separation in marriage with Assemblies had changed just a bit ago, and I would be able to keep everything I had and not be concerned. I had been unequally yoked to begin with, but I did not realize just how much unequal thoughts and beliefs were in our marriage. So sad because I gave it 47 years. WOW!

Trouble comes and goes in life. There will be times that you cannot handle it by yourself, but when that time comes, do not hesitate to ask for help, and don't be ashamed to ask God. God, who made you, makes allowances for your weaknesses and He will never exclude you from His love and care. You will be lifted up!

Always remember this, *"When I was in trouble, I called upon the Lord, and He heard me and delivered me from all my fears."* PSM 34:4

As I kept moving forward and doing my Sunday services, I was OK. I had been an only child and really did not need a lot going on. I am not a drama person, but it is so sad to see how the world thinks about some things. So I am moving forward and not afraid.

One Sunday after the service, a gentleman came up to me. He was tall, a little tired, and wanted to receive Jesus. Right before the prayer he told me his mother was a full-blooded Apache Indian. Well, during my young life, all the western movies I saw always portrayed Apache as being very wild, but this man was alone. He told me that he had been living in the woods of Tennessee when a lady came up to his tent and told him that it was time to receive Jesus; so, he decided to leave Tennessee and come to Kentucky.

Somehow, he heard of Harbor House and came to live there for a while. I did not know it would be a short while. He proceeded on to show me a bear claw on his belt and he told me that he wasn't afraid of anything. He said that he was being touched in such a strong way. It was powerful, and he was not afraid, and had never felt this strong touch Spiritually before. We rejoiced and the service was over.

That next week, I got a phone call at work. It was the gentleman who had gotten saved with the bear claw. I did not know that he would be leaving Harbor House so soon. He told me he had reconciled with his family and gotten his job back as an over the road truck driver. He wanted to thank me and let me know about what was going on the Sunday before.

While on the road, he pulled into an " over the road" truck drive-in church. He went over to attend the service. He had not much money and was unable to give but as he was leaving, the preacher called him over and placed some bills in his hand. He was thrilled because he was on his way to the truck stop for a meal. As he sat down, he opened up the money, and there were one hundred dollars. He could hardly hold back the tears with thankfulness. God rejoices over one sinner coming to Him and will supply his needs.

Harbor House

My prayer is that the seedlings that are planted, come in for preparation and some will be unrooted and then rooted into its position. Even in another position, to grow stronger and this is only for a season. I knew that when I spoke, I was speaking to God's seedbed. Some wanted more and some did not.

When you are in a seedbed, you come in at times to water. The Lord says He is the Vinedresser, and every resident that I have spoken to will come forth in a new way, in a new day. God will empower those who cry out to Him for more.

Some of our residents are in the valley of decision with many decisions to make. Desperately needing God's wisdom and plan. Everyone needs a fresh wind of the Holy Ghost. Breaking of curses that will be taken care of. Cutting off your personal purposes so that the purposes of God can come true.

There are things that only Jesus can bring forth. He waits for the real person that you are to come forth. Forces that are for us, are greater than those against us. I prayed breaking every curse and words be broken off my children.

God's wisdom goes deeper into the interior of His purposes within. It is not the latest message, but the oldest. God determines to bring out the best in us. It's in Christ that we find out who we are and what we are living for.

Long before we first heard of Christ and got our hopes up, He had His eye on us and had designs on us for glorious living. Part of the overall purpose He is working out in everything and everyone who will allow Him to shine thru them. If we cannot just stand on His promises but kneel on His promises.

MORE
BLESSINGS TO COME

Earlier in time, when in Aglow we all traveled to Cumberland Gap where Daniel Boone had come thru to open up the west. It was organized by a prophet from Kentucky. It was a three-day meeting with worship being lead on three different levels of the mountain, and we would ride up and down on golf carts to participate. It was a meeting that we would attend to open up the west to the Spirit of God and what He wanted to do.

An Indian chief was there from out west and we gave him gifts and asked to be forgiven for the past. I did not know that a pastor from Manchester, Kentucky was there and was receiving his orders. His county was overtaken by drug and illegal government officials.

It's a long story about how this came to be... Appalachian Dawn, a documentary was put together to show the world how God came to the county and delivered the county of corrupt officials and drug activity. They had already lost several teens from high school and the county of Clay was suffering much. A call to community prayer brought most of the residents to their knees. God changed their water and brought big fish and it is now called "The City of Hope".

I had a community viewing of this documentary in Henderson County and was very pleased with the amount of people who came. After seeing what the Lord had done in Clay county, they prayed over me to have the Apostolic anointing that was on that county to come and be with me for Henderson County.

I felt to go on a sabbatical. A time of quietness, and after being the Harbor House pastor for seven years, I resigned to pursue what the Lord would have me do for the present time for Henderson County. Being a pastor opened up doors for me even in other parts of the State. I became connected with a ministry in Evansville, Indiana, called (DAG) Divine Allowance Gathering. I had wonderful people around me and fellowshipped with a prophetess and her husband was the worship leader.

I got into government places several times in the Spirit. I also got to pray over the police chief of Evansville, IN, the Healing House in Owensboro, Kentucky, Kentucky Prayer Focus, Kentucky Prayer Team, and I would travel to Frankfort occasionally to pray with others in the rotunda. By being connected to the Kentucky Prayer Team, we got to go into the meeting rooms of our government and pray for our leaders.

During my time at Harbor House, I got connected to Teen Challenge of Kentucky and I had them come to the Harbor House to minister to the residents. I was also able to get a friend's son into the home in Dixon, Kentucky. It had only been open a few years, and Teen Challenge is for anyone 18 and over.

This young man had a heart, so he accelerated there and thanked me for helping him. He was employed there awhile and met a wonderful girl and married. He was also able to return to the occupation that he had studied for. I consider him as one of my spiritual sons. I so enjoyed going to his wedding in Owensboro, KY. I pray blessings over this son.

Chad's Hope which is another Teen Challenge home got built in Manchester, Kentucky. This was during the time of the outpouring, and I got to go there on several occasions. One day, I got a call from a gentleman from Manchester, KY, who I had gotten to know, and I had him come to Harbor House to give his testimony.

He had received Jesus in an outhouse on a construction site in the middle of the night, it was winter and very cold. He had just been released from prison and had nowhere to go, but he made it through. He wanted to send someone to me to help. I was always opened to helping others; so, I said, "Yes". So, my next spiritual son was on his way to the mission.

During my last year at Harbor House, this son that I call my spiritual son came into my life. I saw beyond his vision. I did not know his history, but the Lord had me walk with him a while. He had been in good places and bad places. There were charges resting in Kentucky, which I knew not of. He moved to Indiana a short time after to be out of range. But I kept on walking with him.

I saw the kind of man God wanted him to be, and I got to meet with his mother who let me know, I was right on. After a short time, he moved back over close to where his family resides and turned himself in to take care of the past. With the help of his mother, he was able to be sent to Isaiah's House in Willisburg, Kentucky to serve his time. He was able to take a year program for his sentence. He made use of his time there for the good and worked for the Kingdom of God.

After one year, when released he had a desire to go deeper into the word of God. He got married and went to Campbellsville University, in Campbellsville, Kentucky, where he took theology classes. He was also employed by the college along with his wife.

After a short period of time, he was asked to be the pastor of Asbury Methodist Church there in Campbellsville. I have been blessed to visit a couple of times, and sure plan to go back. The last service I was in, he asked me to say a few words, and of course, I let them know that they had really asked the right person to oversee their flock.

I had an older gentleman come up to me on that day to say that all of his years in church, he had learned more under this pastor than any other. Well, that blessed me so much, I had to have another hug when leaving for home.

I pray blessings over this son.

During this same time, my oldest granddaughter would come on Friday night to visit each week. She came to visit with her great grandmother and of course, me, her grandmother. She would spend the night and sleep with me. My mother, her great grandmother would always come into the room to kiss us goodnight.

Somewhere during this time, my granddaughter had received Jesus. We would talk, play games, and watch Barbie. Then one Friday night she got my Bible and said she was going to preach. She would stand up in front of us, open her bible, and she always went to Genesis...In the beginning, and she did this for several weeks.

Then one particular night was somehow different. After she finished her preaching, it was not long until bedtime. As we had settled down for the night, my mother came in as usual. She leaned down to kiss her great-granddaughter, and as she did, my granddaughter began to pray. My mother looked at me, and both of us, of course, was rejoicing inside. She continued on for 30 minutes, and I mean 30 minutes nonstop. It was amazing, for she never repeated herself. It was precious and right on with the word of God.

While she was reading and preaching out of the Bible, the Spirit must have been leading in a way that I had never seen in a 10-year-old girl. Hearing out of the heart of a little child. Shortly thereafter, I was able to participate in her baptism. She was slain in the Spirit at a church in Madisonville during this time as well. I was overjoyed in my heart and spirit.

I pray blessings over my granddaughter.

CHAPTER FIVE

LOOKING BACK BUT MOVING FORWARD

During this time, I began to reach out to the other ministries that came along before me, and Healing House's apostolic lady minister was very helpful. The West Kentucky Prayer Focus had been established, and there were pastors who felt the shift, and really needed help with the direction to go. We traveled to many places together from cities to valleys. The Lord gave words of direction to lift up pastors on their journey.

The apostolic lady pastor of Word and Spirit, Owensboro, KY was a true blessing to me. Aglow had also opened me up to the prophetic and apostolic leading and I was very comfortable in that call. I understood what it was and what could come in every meeting. That lasted several years. We want to see the Kingdom of God established on earth. May God bless her always.

THE ZEAL OF GOD HAS CONSUMED ME

IT BURNS WITHIN MY SOUL

A DRIVING FORCE THAT CAN NOT BE STOPPED

A FIRE THAT CAN NOT BE QUENCHED

As the Lord's prayer says, "Thy Kingdom come thy will be done on earth as it is in Heaven." There is another place we can walk on this earth. I knew I was operating through the courts of Heaven.

As time seemed to move forward, I began to think about getting back in church. My oldest son and his family had started going to a church not far from where I live. I knew the pastor and had already thought about going there. I kept on with my tax office and felt that my energy level was good enough to carry on. I am not a couch potato and retirement is not in the Bible.

2 Corinthians 4:16-18

16 For which cause we faint not, but though our outward man perish, yet the inward man is renewed day by day

17 For our light affliction, which is but for a moment, worketh for us a far more exceeding and eternal weight of glory

18 While we look not at the things which are seen, but at the things which are not seen: for the things which are seen are temporal; but the things which are not seen are eternal.

I began to think back at the viewing at South Middle School in Henderson. I organized the documentary "The Appalachian Dawn" and how Clay County Kentucky had received divine restoration. When I see God do something in another part of the state, I want to see that happen for Henderson County. I want to see God Glorified in this county. So, I began to feel that I was to write a letter to the local newspaper and thank this community for their participation. There were really a large number of pastors there. I was so thankful.

'United we stand' never more true

Editor:

I want to express my gratitude to all those who came out for the "Appalachian Dawn" viewing in Henderson a few weeks ago at South Middle School. It has been documented as to how the community in Clay County and the city of Manchester came together to raise the quality of their county. It will all be viewed worldwide next year and has been put together by a professional production ministry.

Two pastors came together to pray for their community and ask God to do what only he could do. Many people stepped up and said "yes" and wanted a move of God. It can only be done with unity and heart to seek the betterment of the community God's way. Then God will visit.

After visiting this city the first of this month, I was able to see firsthand that I wanted what that county had. And I will always believe that Kentucky and Henderson County is on the heart of God to raise us to a new level. Let it be in Henderson as it was in Manchester. After their God visit, their water and wildlife were even advanced to better quality and quantity.

The United Way has signs around town that say "Live United." This is a word that we all should take seriously. There is much power in unity when all come together as a voice. Instead of isolating ourselves, we need to venture out of our church walls and see what God is doing all around our city. There will come a day when we will all need each other. To look at each other and know that we are brothers and sisters joined in the faith and want the best for Henderson County.

Our state flag reads, "United we stand and divided we fall." Oh how true. I have so much respect and faith in those who hold the offices of our city and county. Those who did not make it into the political arena also need to be commended as they worked hard. Dr. James Buckmaster worked so hard to reach out even across this state and did a wonderful job. And a special salute to Sheriff Ed Brady after seeing the picture in the paper of the marijuana plants being destroyed in this county.

The further changing that we need can only come through us, and what Jesus has planned for Henderson. Congratulations to all those who won offices in this county. And may we ask for miracles like the Lord did in Manchester, right here in Henderson, Kentucky. I know God will do his part, if we will do our part.

Pastor Linda Fambrough
Henderson

I received a wonderful card from the newly installed mayor of Henderson County, thanking me for the article in the newspaper. I met another minister in Henderson, and he and his wife stood with me to carry out two law enforcement breakfasts and a pastor's luncheon. We also did lunch at the police department to let them know that they were appreciated very much. I invited a speaker from Manchester, KY who was high in law enforcement to share about what happened in their county and how important it was to allow God into the county.

During this same time, the Help Henderson group of residents in Henderson began to arise. It was brought together by a lady minister and everything really went well. Many people came to Central Park. We also had a prayer tent and gave out free items as well, which went on for two or three years.

Also at this time, I met other pastors and leaders, and we would go to the courthouse courtroom and pray at a certain time each week for God's plan and direction for the county to arise. I was always open to what God had in His plan for me. I began to reach out in my community, and I was invited to attend the Henderson City Citizens Police Academy. I was asked to pray there on several occasions. I really enjoyed it, and I also went the next year along with CERT (Citizens Emergency Response Team).

The next year I attended the Kentucky State Police Citizens Academy, and it was wonderful. I saw hard-working individuals who wanted the right thing done. I have to chuckle when I think of my rides with law enforcement. One night the call went to a neighborhood where an elderly lady needed something checked. She thought someone had been in her garage. I was riding the night shift with a city police officer and I was told I could go in but did not choose to. It was a police matter, not a friendly visit.

Then with the state police, I got to ride one day, and there were two traffic stops out on a highway, so I got to travel at high speed with the officer. Oh My, it was so funny because at one of the stops the guy was going to church and no tickets were given that day. But I got the ride of my life. I even got to drive a police car at high speed as if I was chasing someone. Boy was that fun... Ha Ha!

I also came together with the Kentucky Legislative Prayer Caucus in Frankfort. We got to sit in on meetings of our state government. We had a Jericho March'in the supreme courtroom one morning, and a lady was healed. So I knew then that God was with this state. We signed **A Call to Prayer** for Kentucky on January 10, 2012. It was signed by citizens of the state along with legislators. We had a meeting that day and some of our state officials spoke. One of the officials was a beautiful lady, and I loved what she spoke to the group. I had to go say something to her after the meeting, so I thanked her for her service. And she said to me that she felt as Esther...Live or die she would stand for this state. What a blessing, and very humbling to know we have men and women in our state who stood for God. I'm so happy to know that other women feel the call of women in the Bible such as Esther. WOW!

A CALL TO PRAYER FOR KENTUCKY

*T*HROUGHOUT THE HISTORY OF THE UNITED STATES, ITS CITIZENS HAVE DRAWN STRENGTH, HOPE, AND GUIDANCE BY PRAYER AND HUMBLE PETITION BEFORE A LOVING AND MERCIFUL CREATOR—IMPLORING HIM TO WATCH OVER THIS NATION, ITS LEADERS, AND HER PEOPLE.

THE FAITH-BASED PRINCIPLES THAT ESTABLISHED AMERICA, INCLUDING THE FIRST AMENDMENT TO THE CONSTITUTION, GUARANTEE THE FREEDOM OF RELIGION AND ITS EXPRESSION. THE MORAL AND SOLEMN RESPONSIBILITY OF THOSE ELECTED TO PUBLIC OFFICE, DRAWS MANY SERVANTS WHO BELIEVE IN THE POWER OF PRAYER—TO SEEK HUMILITY IN GOVERNANCE, WISDOM IN DECISION-MAKING, COURAGE IN TIMES OF TESTING, AND PROVIDENCE FOR GOD'S FAVOR AND BLESSING.

ON MAY 24, 1774, WHEN FACING ENORMOUS CHALLENGES, CAUCUS MEMBERS FROM THE VIRGINIA HOUSE OF BURGESSES PASSED A RESOLUTION SETTING APART A DAY OF "FASTING, HUMILIATION, AND PRAYER." IN EARLY 2005, A SMALL GROUP FROM THE U.S. HOUSE OF REPRESENTATIVES BEGAN MEETING IN ROOM 219 OF THE UNITED STATES CAPITOL TO PRAY FOR OUR NATION. THE GRAVITY OF THIS MEETING WAS DERIVED FROM THE HUMBLE AND SINCERE BELIEF THAT GOD COULD HEAL AND RESTORE AMERICA. SOON THEREAFTER, THESE MEMBERS FORMED THE CONGRESSIONAL PRAYER CAUCUS TO VIGILANTLY WATCH OVER AND PROTECT THE RIGHT OF INDIVIDUALS TO PRAY.

WE STAND AT THE THRESHOLD OF ANOTHER SIGNIFICANT CROSSROAD: EITHER TO ACKNOWLEDGE AND EMBRACE THE VIBRANT CHARACTER OF OUR SPIRITUAL HERITAGE OR TO PLUNGE HEADLONG INTO THE POSTMODERN VOID—A VALUE-NEUTRAL AND AMORAL VACUUM THAT ENDEAVORS TO DECONSTRUCT MUCH OF WHAT WE HOLD SACRED.

CENTURIES AGO, THE BIBLE RECORDS IN 2 CHRONICLES 7:14 THAT GOD TOLD KING SOLOMON:

"If my people who are called by my name will humble themselves and pray and seek my face and turn from their wicked ways, then I will hear from heaven, will forgive their sin and will heal their land."

WITH CLEAR VISION AND THE RECENT RE-AFFIRMATION OF "IN GOD WE TRUST" AS OUR NATIONAL MOTTO, IT BECOMES MORE EVIDENT HOW IMPORTANT PRAYER IS TO THIS COUNTRY AND TO KENTUCKIANS. THE PREAMBLE OF THE STATE CONSTITUTION HUMBLY ASSERTS, "WE, THE PEOPLE OF THE COMMONWEALTH OF KENTUCKY, GRATEFUL TO ALMIGHTY GOD FOR THE CIVIL, POLITICAL AND RELIGIOUS LIBERTIES WE ENJOY, AND INVOKING THE CONTINUANCE OF THESE BLESSINGS, DO ORDAIN AND ESTABLISH THIS CONSTITUTION."

THE PATRIOTISM OF THE COMMONWEALTH'S FIRST GOVERNOR, ISAAC SHELBY, HELPED INSPIRE THE STATE MOTTO, "UNITED WE STAND, DIVIDED WE FALL." FURTHERMORE, THE OFFICIAL LATIN COMMONWEALTH MOTTO, ADOPTED IN 2002, AFFIRMS, "DEO GRATIAM HABEAMUS" (LET US BE GRATEFUL TO GOD).

WE, THE UNDERSIGNED BELIEVE IN PRAYER AND THE JUDEO-CHRISTIAN PRINCIPLES THAT REMIND US THAT OUR RIGHTS COME FROM ALMIGHTY GOD, UNITE IN THIS PROCLAMATION. ACCORDINGLY, THIS DAY WE RESPECTFULLY AND HUMBLY ISSUE A "CALL TO PRAYER" FOR THE COMMONWEALTH OF KENTUCKY AND INVITE KENTUCKIANS EVERYWHERE TO PRAY THAT GOD WILL CONTINUE TO BLESS THIS COUNTRY, OUR NOBLE STATE AND THE FREEDOM FOR WHICH THEY STAND.

*W*ITNESS THE FOLLOWING SIGNATURES OF ELECTED OFFICIALS OF THE STATE OF KENTUCKY AS OF THE 10TH DAY OF JANUARY IN THE YEAR OF OUR LORD, 2012.

I was asked to join the Congressional Prayer Caucus formed in Washington, D.C.

I was kept up to date with the needs of this country. That was awesome. I made a declaration over this state: DECLARING OVER THIS COUNTY THAT GOD WANTS CHANGE IN FOUR AREAS.

{100}

CHURCH, GOVERNMENT, EDUCATION, AND COMMERCE. I believe the Lord spoke that to me. I do not know the needs of these four areas, but God does.

There were words spoken forth over this state from Jerusalem in 1999. I do not remember who spoke forth, but it was awesome. I do know that there are forces wanting the Lord, prayer, and the Ten commandments to be taken out everywhere. How horrible is that? And with abortion and same-sex marriage, it is no wonder America struggles. I cannot understand how two men, or two women can play the part of a mom and dad. It puts the children in total confusion, and they cannot produce as God desires.

BUT GOD, BUT GOD, BUT GOD IS STILL IN CONTROL!!!!!!!!!!!!!!

My dear cousin Marsha had a heart for the unborn, it would be so happy to know that Marsha's Place has grown, and many are being helped because of her obedience. She did not get to see it, but if God allows, she may know of its success. There are also other needs that I am sure of here in Henderson County. Parents with children don't always seem to be doing the right thing for their children in this day in which we live.

Sometimes we get just enough light for the step we are on. We have to stop looking at what was and look at what can be. Most things in life have to be worked for, but some people don't want to put forth no effort. Have you ever had something good turn out from something bad? Instead of all the things you do not know, think on what you do know. Instead of pondering on the past, set your course for the future. ALLOW GOD TO BE THE CAPTAIN OF YOUR SHIP. DIVE IN, DIVE IN WHEN YOU NEED TO.

The Kingdom of God is wherever it is responded to. The Bible can always be trusted to be correct. I want you to know that the King James can be understood because it is by the Spirit when you read and are serious about applying it to your life. The way it speaks, it is also a prophetic book that applies to today and the future.

A few years ago, I came in contact with a group out of Texas. It was a group of rodeo stars and others who wanted to show Jesus at the rodeos and other places they traveled to perform. I was amazed because of me being a western rider in my earlier life and having several quarter horses, they were breeding especially to produce white quarter horses. You never hardly ever see a white quarter horse. They are on the internet as Glory Riders, Joy West, and they are still moving forward.

I got very close to their headquarters in 2001 while at an Aglow meeting in Dallas but did not end up having time to go. They are putting a lot of effort into horses and beauty to bring God's glory and others to the reality that there would be a King returning on a white horse. They would ride in the arena, and the one in front would be standing up on his horse dressed as Jesus. God bless those people.

Unbeknown to me, my first horse was a white horse. I had no clue what the Bible said about white horses. It was not a quarter horse, but it was white. I think of them ever so often, and wish they were in our area. Their message was, **YOU KNOW WHO YOU ARE IN CHRIST, SO LET YOUR LIGHT SHINE!**

I was speaking to one of my family members one day, and she shared that she was a Daughter of the American Revolution. This sounded very interesting, so I was invited to their next meeting. It was a luncheon, and as I sat down, I began to have tears as I looked around at these older women still standing for a cause. When asked if I would like my heritage searched, I said, yes.

It took about a year or more, but it finally came to fruition with help from Washington. It was through my grandfather's line on my dad's side. When I was presented with my papers and credentials, they spoke these words. "We are so happy to present you with this certificate as proof that your grandfather fought for our freedom." Then I knew why all the tears because I was connected by my grandfather of days gone by.

The grandfather of the Revolutionary War was First Sgt. to George Rogers Clark. He had been given 200 acres for his service as our country had no money in Boxville,

KY, where he lived until his death. That told me that the United States government cared and respected him and his service.

He is buried on that land in Union county, and a state marker is raised for his recognition on the corner where the two county roads meet. His service was in Kentucky near Cincinnati. His grave is covered with vines of ivy, I have been told. He was a pioneer. You can also be a pioneer in the spiritual realm as well, when the Lord wants change, we have to be faithful and willing to help make the change.

A little earlier, I became connected to the history of a woman who is buried in this county. She is from Georgia, but her son brought her here after the death of her husband. She was a true warrior and there is a picture hanging somewhere in our courthouse and she is named in front of our courthouse. A busload of people came to Henderson a few years ago to check it out where she was, thinking that they might take her back to Georgia, but no they did not. She is in a family plot on a farm.

There are many things named for her in Georgia, a park, a highway, and several other things. I was invited to Georgia for a celebration of her life and accomplishments, but I did not get to go. During the Civil War, which was the next war in Georgia when the men were away the women armed themselves because of this pioneer and patriotic lady. She had killed and hung the enemy in the earlier war and was a smart cookie. So other women knew that they could protect their land. In fact, when the enemy came, he backed away from these women.

During the later years of this pioneer, she gave her heart to Jesus, and waged war on the enemy of our souls and did damage to the evil of this world. She is so amazing and carried out her mission in life. Thank You, Jesus!

I had a few years of busy travel but had begun going to a new church and I found it to be fulfilling. The word was preached, and the music was good. Being an Assembly of God minister, I always walk thru what doors are opened to me. The pastor would ask me to do an occasional service, and there was a sweet dear lady who came to most services and gave out tongues in the congregation. Being a minister and knowing what the word says about interpretation, when the Lord moved on me, I began to give that interpretation.

The Lord was also calling me into another arena. In 2016, the Kentucky Prayer Focus had organized a statewide Bible read from the originator from Somerset, KY. Henderson County would be standing with 120 counties that would be reading the same verse at the same time, beginning on New Year's Day.

Kentucky has been called the Upper Room state. I went to my new pastor, and he said he would stand with me. I prayed about it and decided that Central Park in Henderson would be the ideal place. It would be in the center of the county. The Lord had called me as a watchman over this county along with another sister here in the county a long time ago. So, I began to pray about who needs to come alongside me, and the Lord brought to my mind other pastors that He wanted to join with me to bring this forth.

It was awesome. It was in the 20s for the temperature outside, but we did what we could. I got a call one day from a dear friend saying he wanted to read the Bible in Central Park during the Bible reading. He said that he had cancer and did not know how long God would keep him here on the earth, but he was able to drive and get to the park. I said, of course, come right on. He actually came twice to read. We got wonderful coverage in the newspaper for two years, but the local newspaper made drastic changes, and the new man did not work with me. BUT GOD is still in control.

That Bible read lasted several days. A little later into the summer, my friend that was sick with cancer, who had come to the park to read called me again and said, "Linda, we have to do preaching in the park. The children of this county are in serious need and are suffering. I need you to put it together and speak and I will arrange others to speak, along with who you want also. God has given me a call and I have a message for this county."

Of course, I was thrilled to see him being busy about his Father's business. He certainly wanted to be faithful. So I began to put PREACHING, PRAYER, AND PRAISE TOGETHER to be held in the month of September and again in Central Park. At New Beginnings we carried our Sunday evening services to the park.

When the first service in Sept. came, my friend came in a wheelchair along with his family. He was a lot weaker, but he had a message. He spoke out into the atmosphere and into the wind of Henderson county and to all those who were seated at the gazebo. We asked the Lord to send it where it needed to go, from the north to south and east to west.

My friend passed away a few weeks after this meeting, and we all miss him very much. I know he is busy preparing the horses for Jesus. He loved horses, and that is what Jesus needs right now. This friend was the most educated person I ever knew when it was discussed about Israel.

We are continuing to speak into the county with our services and music. This will be the fifth year in 2020. We desire God's will in this county. We are in the middle of a virus with much separation, and it is June, but we keep pressing on. God knows all about it, and He knows the heart of this county and can hear what is being preached and prayed for.

The next year, the Lord told me to continue on. My pastor spoke along with the other pastor that I had asked for that particular evening. It was next to the last Sunday night in September at the park. As the service was about to close, I walked over to the two pastors, and as I looked out into the park, I saw rain falling. It was a beautiful sunshiny evening. As I began to look longer at the rain, I realized it was from heaven and it was falling as crystals. Well, I got overly excited. I could tell no one saw this but me. I have never been too excited. I knew that God had heard us and was honoring us in this hour.

I began to feel a little funny on the inside that night, but I just waited it out but decided to go to the emergency room on Tuesday. They checked me out and found nothing and said you can go home or be admitted and have a stress test in the morning. Well, that sounded ok... I thought that I would just go home. Except, I could not continue on without knowing what was wrong. So, I laid my purse back down and told them I would stay.

They had already hooked me to a lot at this time in the hospital, and as they came to transport me to a room, they began to say, "She is in the middle of a heart attack!" They saw it on the computer, but I had no pain. And to this day, I have never had any pain. This was 5 o'clock on a Tuesday when I got to my room, and I had no idea what to expect. All I got was doctor visits. Seeing a person's heart attack on a computer just staggers my mind, since it was me that they were looking at.

On Thursday afternoon, the surgeon came in with the doctor, and the doctor wanted a triple bypass. But the surgeon said no, she only needs two stents, and the rest can be treated. They said, "We will see you in the morning to discuss this and decide what to do." They had already looked inside of my heart earlier, and I was blessed to see one of my clients who was assisting the doctor doing the procedure. I have clients everywhere, so thankful.

So, the day was over, and I wanted to rest and pray. I really needed the Lord in this hour, as it was totally out of my hands. I was thankful as I was anxious for nothing. I knew God had me in the palm of His hand.

I seemed to be resting well and had fallen asleep only to be awakened by the hustle and bustle of nurses coming into the room. They began to hook me up with even more cords of different things. I looked at the clock and it was 2 a.m. I asked what was going on because I was having no pain. The nurse said, that when they see any of their patients with this reading, you are in a heart attack and we go into lifesaving mode. We will also be calling your sons. I said, oh please don't call my sons, please wait until at least 6 a.m. Then they carted me off.

It was all done thru my thigh. I don't know how long I was down there, but as they finished and began to roll me back to my room, the nurse that helped me said, "Well, I believe you got your answer." She meant what procedure would be for me. I knew exactly what she meant. The Lord had taken care of what procedure He wanted for me. It's hard to understand when you see your heart attack on a computer and have no pain. Thank you, Jesus!

As I returned to my bed, I had to lay flat for nine hours and that was the roughest part of it. As I began to think, pray, and thank God for what had been done, the Lord began to speak, "I AM NOT DONE WITH YOU, IT IS NOT YOUR TIME."

WOW! The Lord has more for me to do and I knew I could do everything He asked. The crystal rain from Heaven was just too exciting and overwhelming. The doctor told me they were going to keep me for three days longer for rest only. Do whatever, but rest.

Not long before this, I had done my cousin's funeral, and I had made two trips to Florida alone, and two trips with my oldest son and family to care for her and her needs. I had to put her in a nursing home, and at her death I had her sent back to Kentucky. I had a lot going on in 2016 and must have gotten overloaded and did not realize it.

I was unable to find her son, who lives on the streets of Evansville, Indiana. But within the next few months I was able to connect with him. He rides a bicycle and has to eat at rescue missions or churches. I just don't understand, but one thing for sure, he excepted Jesus as his Savior and took off his hat with reverence.

My life was beginning to get back to normal or at least beginning to recover with strength. I began to ponder on the tax office, I had worked far beyond what most people do in years. The Lord had put me in this work, in the government of this earth and I enjoyed every moment of it. Even when I went to work at 4 a.m. to cover the work for the day I always gave my client's my personal attention. So, I prayed and told the Lord, I felt I might be ready to retire. I did not hear anything from Him at that time. He knew I was pondering that in my mind and in my heart and I would not stop without His word. I don't even remember when I began to think about it, but one morning at 4 a.m. I was awakened by the Master to say, "I AM RELEASING YOU FROM THIS WORK. YOU CAN RETIRE. BUT I'M NOT DONE WITH YOU!"

As I began to think about it, I could see that 2019 would be my 50th year of working as a tax person. I began to put my last days in the office together, and it all worked out well. I miss my wonderful clients; some had been with me for 30 years. I had seen them grow, blossom, mature, and branch out and become everything God wanted for them. Some of my clients have been able to bless me in other ways.

But most of all, friendship is so important, and seeing these clients appreciate me is so strong. We all have a journey, but God has a destiny for us all. It has been such a wonderful journey and sharing it with others. I pray God's blessing on all my previous clients and blessings on my associate of many years. I was so happy to have a Christian girl to come alongside, someone who was worthy of growing inside my company.

Bless you always P.

As I began to think about the sale of the building where my tax office was, I began to get a good look at what was in crates and in the bookcases in the back of the building. I had used it for storage and had so much that I had to rent a storage unit to clear out the building because I had no room at home. As I began to look at my material and ministry items, I was blown away, I had thirty years of precious papers. A dear client had given me an office space to also use for my personal items. Thank you, Jesus! Thank you, dear client, God Bless You!

Time was moving on, and I was adjusting to this newness in my life. I was so thankful. One evening, the message at church was a message on the bride, "Not to dirty her garment." Well, God will not allow her garment to be dirty, but it was a good message. So much so, that I began to ponder, and meditate on the word and the return of the Messiah. I thought about the church and what condition it was in. I could tell the Spirit was upon me because there was a precious feeling of being thankful that I was a daughter of the King. As I was preparing for bed, it did not seem any different than any other night, but the Lord began to sing to me:

OH!! HOW BEAUTIFUL YOU ARE, TO ME, CAN'T YOU SEE

YOU'RE EVERYTHING I'VE EVER HOPED FOR

YOUR EVERYTHING I NEED

OH!!! HOW BEAUTIFUL YOU ARE, TOO ME

CAN'T YOU SEE, YOUR EVERYTHING I'VE EVER HOPED FOR AND EVERYTHING I NEED

AND OH!!! HOW BEAUTIFUL YOU ARE, TO ME

Knowing I was in my right mind, and already having the Lord speak to me and through me earlier in my life. This was an awesome place to be, in the presence of a Holy God that desired to sing to me. It was of a different time and different place, even though I was here on this planet, I was truly seated in Heavenly places, and I knew I was a true daughter of the King. I meant something to Him, He heard me and saw me in this life and would be faithful to me. I humble myself at His visits.

My second granddaughter was coming into this life, and after a very hard delivery for her and her mother, she was put in NICU at the hospital. As hard as it was, God covered them thru it all and everything has gone well. My understanding is, she has been released from the heart doctor and was asked a short time back to be the Ambassador for the March of Dimes in Evansville, Indiana. She was dedicated to God at their church a while back, and I am excited to see what God has planned for her. I hope I will be around to see at least a part of it.

I was over visiting this granddaughter, my youngest son, and daughter-in-law one day at their home, and we had a good visit. I was preparing to go home when my daughter-in-law said she had a headache and had it most of the day. I asked if I could pray, and I did. After the prayer, I put my arms around my daughter-in-law and pulled her to me. As I stood with her in my arms, my five-year-old granddaughter says, "That was Beautiful."

I was so amazed that a five-year-old child could see beauty, as it was from God. Suffer not the little children to come unto Me. It really hit me spiritually to know that God was with this child, and He may be giving and showing her things we know not of. Just as He did me as a small child.

God's blessings upon this granddaughter.

It is such a beautiful day
Our new little daughter is on her way
Being sent on the Wings of a Dove
Also bringing God's steadfast love.

For God's Love is being shed abroad in your heart
So from Jesus, never, never depart
My love will keep you safe from harm
So lean on Me and My strong arm
Lift up your prayers unto my ears
For I am one who will always hear.

For this is a new day
We are to walk in a new way
The way of total obedience is the way it should be,
Because in Jesus you can be set free
Free to love and live with life's best
And forsaking evil and all the rest
For only in God's love is there love, fire and light
Because He dwells within and gives what is right.

So enjoy this day regardless of what you hear
Because I am in the land to deliver her from all her fear
I am walking in your space and I walk at a different pace
So love Me with every ounce of your being
As I am the Soon Coming King.

...

It was given to Linda Fambrough by the Lord thru the Holy Spirit
on Sunday morning November 11, 2001

{115}

We have a new pastor and youth pastor. They are precious and mean a lot to me. There are a few people in this church who have received the Baptism of the Holy Ghost, and the Lord is beginning to use them as well. It is a desire to see the people all pray at the same time in whatever tongue they choose; spirit or natural. At least that is what I am feeling. Our church family is moving on and we are growing.

I had to put my mother in a nursing home last year. She has no feeling from the waist down. I kept her at home as long as I could, even after having two doctors from two different rehabs say, earlier in time that she needs to go in a home for care. But I said, no, I will do it as long as I can. But that day came, and with hardly any motor, and having to be lifted from bed to chair, I just could not do it. The home where she is at is just wonderful. Mother is really at home while being away from home.

I am so blessed today, as every day. I got a mail out by the nursing home. It is a book, where they went to the residents and asked for their wisdom and then they published the book. My mother took part, and so her part is being included also in my book. Her book is called, Words of Wisdom.

My mother knows I am writing a book but won't this be a surprise. God is blessing us again! We used the virus time for good and I have been able to move forward at a much faster pace since the virus came along. So, not all time was wasted. I'm sure a lot of people used this time for the Lord.

Redbank's went to the residents that wanted to give their wisdom. I am sure this took much time.

My mother's Words of Wisdom:

RELATIONSHIPS: Be honest, talk to each other, trust, and have God with you both.

RAISING KIDS: Put them in church. Love them when they do wrong.

FAITH: Make sure you go to church. Always have faith and God in your life.

HAPPINESS: Smile always, love always, give hugs, and always be nice to everyone.

WORK ETHIC: Do the best you can. Always have a smile, use manners.

I want to add another one.

When you are cooking for others, always do it with love.

Printed May 2020 by Redbanks, where many residents put in a contribution with their Words of Wisdom. Such a wonderful idea. God bless you Redbanks.

The virus of 2020 still has Redbanks on lockdown. I haven't seen my mother for several months and it is now July. Time is moving on; we live in a different day. Things are changing and a little unusual.

When the Lord told me to write a book over a year ago, I had to give it time to soak in. I just was not sure, but God does not leave you alone when He has a plan, and He desires you to walk in it. After having another word spoken to me, I knew I had to go for it. He would not have told me to do it if I could not. The only books I was around were government books that I would look up answers for different tax issues. I had to chuckle because the Bible is a government book. There are courts in heaven, I had been taught this several years ago and I know the Bible is even more important in the day we live.

It is so important what you think and what action you take with the Holy Ghost. God sent the Holy Ghost on the day of Pentecost to the upper room where His children were waiting to be endued with power, that they knew not of; but they waited. Some in the present day have no patience.

The Holy Ghost carries out the plans of God. Even Jesus breathed on the disciples before He left this earth to receive the Holy Ghost in the last chapter of John. Jesus knew what was ahead, and that the disciples and people in the upper room needed to be as strong as God wanted. They had a work to carry out.

This was the beginning of the church. Are we carrying out God's will and plan? We must step up to the plate and carry the gospel to all people and be a light in this dark world. The Lord has really been speaking about the book of Jude. It is the last book before Revelations. How we are to be watching for false teachers and their influence within the churches. It challenges all believers to rise up and earnestly contend for the faith which was once delivered to the saints. That is why reading the Bible for yourself is so important. God will teach you. And please pray in faith to be filled with the Holy Ghost.

Life is what's ahead, not what is behind.

Success is getting up one more time.

When things go wrong, don't go with them.

God can mend all broken hearts; you just have to give Him the pieces.

I don't have to attend every argument I'm invited to.

Our eyes have been placed in front because it is more important to look ahead than look back.

I have seen the mercy of God.

Most people will be about as happy as they decide to be.

Success stops when you do.

When your ship comes in, make sure you are willing to unload it.

I have been overwhelmed by God's love and I will not exchange that for anything. I was put in perfect rest years ago, and nothing remains to hold me back. At Brownsville, I was released to dance in a way that I never knew, and in my later years with less strength, I still dance inside.

Don't underestimate your God. The independent nature keeps you from the real need of the Spirit. You must tarry until you be endued with power. The power is given when you receive the Baptism of the Holy Ghost with the evidence of tongues. I waited a while before I told my family, God forgives me. Our flesh has to decrease, and some just do not understand that.

The Lord told me that my life was a treasure and that there was much gold because much Love of God had been poured into me. Be not weary in well-doing, be ready to perform my word. The word is alive in us and wants to move through us. We have to surrender who we are to become what God wants us to be. Bringing forth fruit, for you are not a weed. You are called to be blessed, not rejected. God's word is promises, not just a dreamer.

As a child you are profitable. The Lord is appointing people of the region to saturate the earth. People of the Spirit, Walking in the Spirit, a kingdom greater than we have known. The Lord spoke to me, "Neither will you be denied. Neither will your sons be denied. First in the natural, and then in the Spirit." We are glory in physical form. Spirit does not go through the mind. The heart is also spiritual. PRAISE GOD, HE HAS MY CHILDREN COVERED. As I have said many times, He does not make mistakes, and He does not make JUNK.

We are in different days at this time, looking unto Jesus, leaning on Jesus, and learning of Jesus. I had already been in an intense time in the Spirit. I had put my ministry upon a shelf until I felt I could handle it. God is patient, Thank The Lord. I was brought totally into His will. I did not really know that could be done. My mind said I had totally missed it, but my heart is fixed, Oh God, My heart is fixed. All was forgiven, God is good, ALL THE TIME.

We have to have a vision and allow God to move us from an old familiar place, into His will for purpose. Resist bad thoughts and crucify any area that is contrary to His word. Jesus wants to see an expression of our faith. The Lord is a God of the second chance. I love the scripture, *"You will be a city set on a hill that cannot be hidden."*

The Bible speaks of our foundations being laid by sapphires. Sapphire is my birthstone. I am so thrilled to know that God is not done with me or America.

We want to become the dwelling place of God. Everyone who believes in Christ Jesus and has received Him as their Savior has obtained an equal privilege of receiving whatsoever the Bible promises. Our God is no respecter of person. The basis of His giving is not determined by a sliding scale of who is, who is not, or when one finally becomes worthy of receiving. To God the Father, a believer is worthy to receive simply because he or she is His own.

God has not made the manifestations of His promise contingent on any of man's conditions. The Lord docs not realign His faithfulness to conform to man's misconceptions of Him. His faithfulness to His promises simply exists because He exists. He is faithful to all He has said. A heart that has been able to receive Him is a heart that is full of Thanksgiving, Understanding, Love, and Worship.

The difference between those who receive from the Lord, and those who do not, is the amount of room the person has allowed inside themselves to receive from Him. Those who receive much have been stripped off, torn down, and moved out the trappings of their old natures, thereby enlarging their capacity to receive. Having done this, they have ceased to oppose themselves and the work of God in their lives.

How much time will you invest in your life? Computers with defective programs produce garbled meaningless messages. When we try to produce Godly character with an unrenewed mind, we find ourselves puzzled by our ungodly actions. God wants to reprogram our way of thinking, and so it means to send out clear messages of His love and power to change lives. Minds have to be renewed. Every sin we commit begins in the mind.

The inner man of our spirit is connected to your vocal cords. Truth is expressed to God in worship. The Holy Spirit is enthusiastic about you. In our normal tendency to think from a negative mindset, we need to repent and think again. Worry, anxiety, fear, anger, bitterness, and resentment will not enable you to become Christlike. A successful relationship with Jesus is founded on Rest, Peace, and Joy for Him.

"God of Heaven Himself will prosper us. He means for us to arise and build." -Nehemiah 1st Chapter

True greatness comes from being everything God wants you to be. I have said many many times, He does not make mistakes, and He does not make Junk. When you have lost your strength, it does not do anything to your hearing. He is revealing His purposes and exposing the flesh so that it can be crucified. Thank you, Lord, for exposing and be with the children of God who live the double life so that we can be conformed to the image of Jesus. No double lives or standards can live in the presence of God.

He is taking all rejection from his children and bringing in man's truth in favor of a more appealing version of the truth from God Himself. Let truth stand and let God arise and all our enemies be scattered. Ask what can you do for your country, not just what your country can do for you. Some people are still babies and want to get instead of giving. They say, feed me, water me, change me, always getting instead of giving. Service to self, rather than to others.

We will defeat the war, we must go through and come out on the other side as the winner, thereby winning the war. We must be God's secret service, slaying the giants that seem to come our way and not allowing anything to stand in the way of God's plan for our lives.

It has been said that the revival will not be what we might think. Not only in the miraculous and supernatural, but God's birthing will be a place where the awe and fear of God saturates the atmosphere like a cloud to those who are pure of heart. I will not be fearful even though the fear of God will permeate it. Joy will erupt in all of us and we must come to a new level of purity of heart.

Have you ever thought about life maintenance? Take the GOSPEL daily, or if you're going on a journey, before you travel you think about what you are going to drive... will it make the trip?

Consider the demands of the journey and pack accordingly:

Cold weather... take a jacket.

Business meeting... take a laptop.

Family trip... take sneakers and clothing.

God does the same with us, He purposed us in His heart to be packed for the purpose. He looks at our entire life and determines your assignment and has given you the road map to accomplish what you are to do.

> » By the miracle of His life in us and with us, we will realize our greatest achievements.

> » Success stops when you do, so don't let your past hold your future hostage.

> » When your dreams are dying. His plans are often just beginning.

> » Everyone needs restoration, God does not just want visitation, He wants habitation.

> » Trials and testing in life will make you bitter or better. With Jesus, it is always better.

» The wilderness is not permanent, so don't get stuck.

SO HERE IT IS GOD. I HAVE FULFILLED THIS JOURNEY AND GLORY TO YOUR NAME!

As a believer, I have the privilege of receiving Spiritual wisdom, power, authority, understanding, answers, and peace right now. My Heavenly Father has no desire to withhold any good thing from me. I have the good things from my Father now and I do not oppose myself.

Isaiah 55:11-13,

[11] *"So shall my word be that goeth forth out of my mouth. It shall not return unto me void, But it shall accomplish that which I please and it shall prosper in the thing where to I sent it."*

[12] *"For ye shall go out with joy, and be led forth with peace. The mountains and the hills shall break forth before you into singing, and all the trees of the field shall clap their hands."*

[13] *"Instead of the thorn, shall come up the fir tree, and instead of the brier shall come up the myrtle tree, and it shall be the Lord for a name, for an everlasting sign, that shall not be cut off."*

Psalms 24:7-10,

7"Lie up your heads, O ye gates, and be ye lifted up, ye everlasting doors, and the King of Glory shall come in."

8"Who is this King of Glory, The Lord strong and mighty, The Lord mighty in battle."

9"Lift up your heads O ye gates even lift them up, Ye everlasting doors and the King of Glory shall come in."

10"Who is this King of Glory, The Lord of Host, he is the King of Glory, Selah."

Father, I ask for a release of your kingdom. A release in the Spirit so that your body can go beyond. I ask for a release in the gifts. I ask for increased anointing over Henderson County and Kentucky. Create this body of believers for your pleasure. Give them Godly creativity, and bring the personality of this city, county, and state into alignment with your divine will. IN JESUS' NAME.

Lord, as I look back over the last few months in writing this book, I will never be able to express the beauty of your holiness. It has been an honor and a privilege to write these words, and really not even know where the Lord would take me.

What I have cannot be taken away from me by no one. My children and their families are covered by the blood of Christ and will go with the rapture. God only knows what will be hereafter that, and I do not desire my children, spiritual sons, and foster sons to be left behind.

I trust that my story will help someone. To give hope in the place of confusion and to know that you can do all things through Christ. When I look at where the Lord has taken me, I am very humbled. I want to encourage women who have a calling to know that God will work it out, just do not wait 20 years as I did. Watch for false teachers, and all the world has to offer during this time: such as evil spirits, and other forms of satanic activity. God is not in it.

I learned a long time ago, God is my walker, not my crutch. I was planted, not potted, just to be tossed about. My feet have been fully placed by God. I said a long time ago, I want to touch Him, and I want to know Him more. I went to the river.

I have been so blessed to be associated with those who have an apostle and prophetic callings. It has taught me so much and I am so honored. I have been in prayer with many, many, across this state and it is an honor. I pray this book will be a blessing to encourage others and to look at their lives with thanksgiving and appreciation at whatever level they are at.

Psalm 145:4

"One generation shall praise thy works to another, and shall declare thy mighty acts."

LET THE WORDS OF MY MOUTH, AND THE MEDITATION OF MY HEART BE PLEASING TO YOU EVERYTHING I DO IS FOR THE GLORY OF GOD CONTINUE TO FALL ON ME, LORD.

THE LORD SAID THIS BOOK WILL PREACH. GLORY HAS BEEN HELD BACK BY MAN TO A CERTAIN DEGREE, BUT GOD LOVES HIS DAUGHTERS JUST AS MUCH.

I SPEAK BLESSINGS ON ALL MY SONS AND THEIR FAMILIES. MAY GOD BE WITH THEM AND CARRY THEM WHEN NEEDED. GREATER LOVE IS UPON US THAN THAT OF THIS WORLD.

I SPEAK PEACE, LOVE, JOY UPON MY CHILDREN. GREATER WORKS SHALL YOU DO, AS I WILL GO TO MY FATHER, AND WILL WAIT FOR YOU.

MAY MY CHILDREN LIVE WITH DIVINE PURPOSE. I DECREE AND DECLARE THAT MY CHILDREN SEE HIS GLORY. MAY MY CHILDREN FULFILL THEIR GOD-GIVEN DESTINY? NO OTHER WILL THEY FOLLOW FOR HE IS WORTHY.

AND YOU HAVE A DESTINY!

Dear children

I want my testimony to speak. To my sons, I have done the best I could. I love you so much and desire God to always cover you in all situations. I pray that the peace of God be with you, that you be soft, kind, and loving to your family, and the family to come. May my granddaughters be equipped to live in this world. I have been heir to the grace and goodness of God. He entrusted me with many people, mostly Harbor House young men and Aglow International ministry to women.

I raised my sons in church, and I do not feel that I was worldly religious, or overwhelming. I left their knowledge of God in His hands, as I did not know if I was capable to carry His will and word in the proper way.

As I began to grow and receive my papers with the Assembly of God, I realized that there was a destiny for all of us. I speak God's destiny to my children. Allow God room in your life and you will never be sorry. He is the one who gave you to me. Yes, man plants the seed, but God gives that seed, and the increase of life that comes into a mother's body is eternal.

I am so thankful to be a life-giver and had the birth pains for life to enter into this world. One day you will enter the Kingdom. I pray you know I cared for you with the strength that I had, to strengthen and encourage you at the core of your being.

Even at times, when I did not know what you were going through. I was always there for you when you needed me. I want your heart to be built up in the purposes for which God has called you.

I have shown righteousness, justice, and mercy, and I was a watchman over my 50 years of following the law of the land, speaking to those who wanted my thoughts and direction.

I want my children to receive the knowledge and treasure that only the word of God can give. May God polish your lamp and keep it shining with plenty of oil wherever God has planted you. God has been faithful to me, and I am so blessed and thankful for what He has allowed me to carry in this life. I have my lamp full of oil, and will NOT have the master say, "depart from me," BUT, " Welcome my good and faithful servant, Enter." I have to see a smile on Jesus' face when we meet.

I pray for you often and love you much. May the Lord bless you and pour out His will upon your life as you follow Him. God is calling us to be ready with the stance of a warrior. I felt like a warrior over every obstacle. I have never feared because of the infilling within by Him, the lover of my soul.

May the breath of God blow with a fresh sound with a release of everything that He is over the coming days and years ahead. Sing a new song of redemption, favor, love, and righteousness. A new lightness of spirit. I have aligned my heart with heaven, and I have resounded to the music of heaven with no unbelief.

This world is changing, but God never changes. It will bring a new direction, a new attitude, and all kinds of new organizations, but God is always in control.

Zechariah 2:5

For I, saith the Lord, will be unto her a wall of fire round about and will be the glory in the midst of her.

2:10 Sing and rejoice, daughter of Zion, for lo I come and will dwell in the midst of thee, saith the Lord

Song of Solomon 2:1

I am the rose of Sharon, and the lily of the valleys.

2:2 As the lily among thorns, so is my love among the daughters.

2:3 As the apple tree among the trees of the wood, so is my beloved among the sons. I sat down under his shadow with great delight, and his fruit was sweet to the taste

2:4 He brought me to the banqueting house, and his banner over me was LOVE

Accelerate your love over my children. I have expressed my life as best as I could, and I know that Jesus's life has lived in me. So be blessed and be bold for the Lord our God is with us. He will never leave us or forsake us in the midst of whatever comes our way. He makes a way in the desert and put the spirit of the overcomer within each of us. So we can and will overcome all obstacle that tries to stand in our way. I call down every obstacle that may try to stand in your way and I ask God for His continued blessings upon you, your wives, and your children, and those to come.

I LOVE YOU, Mother

Shalom

AS I THINK ABOUT 2020, THERE ARE GOOD THOUGHTS AND UNHAPPY THOUGHTS, BUT THE BEST THOUGHT IS THAT I FINISHED MY BOOK.

THE UNHAPPY THOUGHTS ARE, MY MOTHER WILL NOT GET TO SEE MY BOOK, UNLESS GOD ALLOWS, SINCE SHE WENT ON TO BE WITH JESUS IN OCTOBER 2020.

I WANT TO DEDICATE THIS BOOK OF TESTIMONY, FIRST TO GOD BE THE GLORY, AND TO MY PRECIOUS SAVIOR JESUS CHRIST. I THANK HIM FOR EVERYTHING.

TO MY PRECIOUS 97 YEAR-OLD MOTHER, WILLIE ANN BROCK, WHO WAS ALWAYS THERE FOR ME, JUST AS I WILL BE THERE FOR MY CHILDREN.

TO MY PRECIOUS CHILDREN, FIRST TO MY OLDEST SON, DARIN FAMBROUGH, WIFE MELISSA, AND MY GRANDDAUGHTER LAUREN, AND MY YOUNGEST SON, JAMES, WIFE KASSIE, AND GRANDAUGHTER KHLOE.

MAY MOTHER AND GRANDMOTHER'S LOVE ALWAYS BE WITH YOU.

MOTHERS DAY

MOTHERS DAY IS HERE, AND I AM FILLED WITH CHEER
WHEN I THINK OF MY PRECIOUS BOYS, MY HEART IS
FILLED WITH JOY

SO THANKFUL FOR THE LOVE THAT COMES FROM ABOVE,
SO STRONG AND PURE AND SURROUNDS US WITH LOVE

AND CAN'T FORGET MY GRANDDAUGHTER, AND THOSE
THAT WILL COME, SEE SHE IS MY GRAND-DAUGHTER
AND SHE IS SO MUCH FUN.

SO I REJOICE IN THIS NEW DAY, AND MAY I NEVER
FORGET, GOD IS THE STRONGEST THING IN MY LIFE
AND YET. I COME AS A LITTLE CHILD, WITH A SMILE
ON MY FACE, FOR I TOO AM RUNNING THIS RACE.

MADE IN HIS LIKENESS, I SET OUT FOR THE KING, AND
THROUGH IT ALL IT IS UNTO HIM I SING
I WILL NEVER LET GO OF MY RELATIONSHIP WITH GOD
AND THANKFUL FOR THE FAMILY THAT HE HAS
ALLOWED ME TO HOLD. THANKING HIM THAT
HE HAS MADE ME BOLD, AND HAS TRULY BROUGHT
ME OUT OF MY MOLD.

MY CHILDREN ARE MOLDED IN HIS SIGHT, AND HE WILL
ALWAYS DO WHAT IS RIGHT. SO STAY CLOSE BY OUR
SIDE, DEAR HEAVENLY FATHER ABOVE, AND CONTINUE
TO SEND DOWN TO US YOUR GLORY AND LOVE
The Lord placed this in my heart on May 1, 2010.
Love,